Praise for Speaking of Death

'Annie offers a compassionate and caring approach to supporting someone through grief, developed through her own experience and the use of expert advice. She emphasises the need for an individual approach in order to face, and manage, the complexities of grief and grieving following a bereavement, yet offers a comprehensive and empathic approach to helping people through the grieving process. She encourages us to face our own fears, such as "upsetting someone more", and to be more aware of grief's complexities and longevity. The book is particularly helpful in suggesting how we can use all our senses to help answer the questions of what is the problem, where is the pain and what can we do to help?'

Shelley Gilbert MBE
CEO Grief Encounter
Daily Mail Inspirational Woman of the Year 2012/13

'It is wonderful. Pitch perfect in tone and a very important book. It will help many people.'

Sally Brampton, author of *Shoot the Damn Dog*

'Wonderfully moving, relevant and important'

Kate Timperley, Maggie's

About the Author

Annie Broadbent is a clinical volunteer at St Christopher's Hospice. She has also trained as a volunteer for 'The Candle Project' – a child bereavement service run by the hospice, and has given talks on supporting the bereaved. She is currently training as a psychotherapist at the Psychosynthesis and Education Trust. In her spare time she writes a blog (www.anniebroadbent.com) about coping with grief and her experiences at the hospice. Annie also writes a monthly online article for *Psychologies* magazine on the taboos surrounding death and grief. This is her first book.

SPEAKING
OF DEATH

WHAT THE BEREAVED
REALLY NEED

ANNIE BROADBENT

piatkus

PIATKUS

First published in Great Britain in 2014 by Piatkus as *We Need to Talk About Grief*
This edition published in Great Britain in 2017 by Piatkus

ISBN 978-0-349-41605-2

Typeset in Sabon by M Rules
Printed and bound by CPI Group (UK) Ltd, Croydon, CR0 4YY

Papers used by Piatkus are from well-managed forests
and other responsible sources.

MIX
Paper from
responsible sources
FSC® C104740

Piatkus
An imprint of
Little, Brown Book Group
Carmelite House
50 Victoria Embankment
London EC4Y 0DZ

An Hachette UK Company
www.hachette.co.uk

www.improvementzone.co.uk

For you Mama

Contents

[...]

Acknowledgements

Thank you to my wonderful agent Jane Turnbull, who recognised the importance of this book, not only for me, but for everyone. She 'got' me right from the start and has been a source of consistent support and encouragement throughout the entire process. Thank you to everyone at Little, Brown for believing in this book, and especially to Claudia Connal and Jillian Stewart, for their magical ability to draw out, even further, the truth in what I'm trying to communicate.

Thank you to Sue James, editor of *Woman and Home* magazine, Fanny Blake and Laura Palmer – three women who went to great lengths to help me get this book published. Their faith in me at such an early stage of the journey really spurred me into action.

Enormous thanks to all the contributors in this book, who generously gave up their time to relive their precious and painful experiences with me, and entrusted me to write their story.

I feel so fortunate for all the people in my life, new arrivals as well as the old timers. Thank you to Bea Addis, who gave up so much to be there for me when Mum died and has cheered me on with such love and faith ever since.

Thank you Dad, for bravely being the initial 'editor' of the first few chapters, and for your limitless and unstinting love, support and encouragement throughout my whole life. It's because of you and Mum that I believed in myself enough to do this. Tommy, my big younger brother – what a thing we have shared together. I'm so grateful it has been you by my side, learning to live without our mum.

And, finally, thank you Mum – for bringing me into this world and for being the kind of person I want to be. You will forever be my greatest inspiration.

Introduction

*At present, death and mourning are treated with much the
same prudery as sexual impulses were a century ago.*

Geoffrey Gorer, anthropologist,
Death, Grief, and Mourning

I was twenty-five when my mum died. I knew she was going to
die. She had had cancer for most of my life. Astonishingly, one
of the things I found hardest about grief was the way in which
people around me responded to it. It seems that death and grief
have become today's taboo. Despite the fact that death is the
only certainty in life, we're all terrified of it – and I don't just
mean terrified of it happening to us, but terrified of seeing it,
talking about it, hearing about it.

Likewise, talking about grief causes anxiety in people. And yet,
again, it is guaranteed that every single person on this planet is
going to experience it in some way or other. Joy, hope, passion –
some might, sadly, never experience these, but we will all lose
someone or something one day, be it a job, a pet, a loved one. And
yet, unlike love or anger, with which we feel confident empathis-
ing, we push grief to one side, and hope that someone else will deal
with it instead. Even when I told people I was writing a book

about grief I noticed them look away or shuffle their feet awkwardly. Few asked why I might be writing such a book, and the conversation was immediately shut down.

This has got to change. In order to support the bereaved, we need to get to grips with death. In my experience, seeing family and friends paralysed by the fear of their own mortality and my grief meant that at times I felt more frustrated and upset about their awkwardness around me than I was about my own loss. You would be right to wonder if occasionally this was actually displaced anger about the death of my mum, and hindsight has taught me that indeed, some of my outbursts back then were more a result of trauma. But people's awkwardness and their consequent absence was real. And it bothered me.

My hope is that the more we talk about death and grief, and the more people share their experiences of what does and doesn't work for them, the less awkward we will all feel about the whole death thing. Then we can build up our capacity to support those who are in mourning.

My way of getting a handle on death and grief was to get right on in there and make it an intimate part of my life. It seemed clear to me after Mum died that the only way to make sense of this terrible thing was to give it meaning somehow. And so I embraced my grief and became a walking, talking, writing bereaved person. I now volunteer at a hospice, helping out in the gym or café and visiting home patients in their final months. I support a child bereavement group and have spoken at 'Death Salons' (social events that bring together independent thinkers who are passionate about subverting death denial), giving tips on how to support other bereaved people and sharing my experience of grief. I'm also training to be a psychotherapist and, of course, I chose to write this book. Talk about 'identifying'.

My personal experience of bereavement, my professional training and my voluntary work have combined to form something of a personal journey, along which I have worked – and continue to work – through my grief, helping me through the lengthy process of overcoming my own fear of death.

This book tells not only my story, but those of fifteen other people who have experienced grief. These people very generously agreed to be interviewed by me and for their story to be shared in order that they may help others. While these stories may well provide solace to anyone in mourning, the book is very much intended as a guide for friends of the bereaved: it is support for the supporters.

Death and Grief: Different Approaches

Following his wife's death, C. S. Lewis wrote in *A Grief Observed*, 'Perhaps the bereaved ought to be isolated in special settlements like lepers.' I know what he meant. It's the pretending that's so frustrating – pretending not to know or notice. I wanted to put a sign outside my house saying, 'Annie's mother has just died; don't ignore this piece of information when you step inside.'

The Victorians got it right by wearing black armbands. 'But don't the bereaved want to be treated like normal people?' you might ask. Well, yes – to a certain extent they do. But that doesn't mean they don't want their new reality to be acknowledged. And the great thing about an armband is that it serves as a warning; it gives the non-bereaved a moment to prepare, so that they approach the person with care and don't automatically respond with the averted gaze and awkward foot shuffle that so often follow on hearing a person explain that someone they love has just died.

Preparation is important, I think. If possible, the non-bereaved need time – even if all that is possible is the briefest moment – to process the information before engaging with the mourner. If you hear about the death directly from the bereaved, then allow yourself to be affected, breathe in the news, take a moment, and then respond from a place of honesty and openness. If you hear about the death indirectly, take advantage of that opportunity to prepare, consider the bereaved, what they're like and how they specifically might be handling the news, before getting in touch. We can never rid grief of its inherent sadness and pain and so, of course, we must allow space for these emotions in the non-bereaved, too. In being prepared, the non-bereaved person has time to silently acknowledge their own emotions without compromising their capacity for support.

In some places, people appear to be much more at ease with death. In Ireland, for example, family and friends of the deceased gather by the body and stay up all night, socialising and remembering. Not much room for hiding, then. In fact, in June 2012 a Grief Awareness Day was launched in Limerick in Ireland, at which a day of talks was organised to empower local people to become actively involved in supporting a community response to loss and grief. Imagine if this was to be emulated elsewhere – if every community in the UK, for example, could find ways to come together and support those of its members who are in mourning.

In Mexico there is a 'Day of the Dead' festival. Every year on this day people celebrate and remember the lives of all their relatives who have died. It's a time for families to get together, share food and recall the good times they enjoyed with their departed loved ones: this often involves playing and dancing to the deceased's favourite music and dressing up as skeletons. While the emphasis is on those who have died, it's the bereaved who are doing the partying, talking and remembering; this, no doubt, has a great knock-on effect on how Mexican society will respond to people who are grieving, reinforcing the fact that grief is not something to fear. Graciela Sanchez, founder of Mexicolore (a UK-based independent teaching team providing specialist educational services on Mexico) says: 'It's amazingly powerful to gather together and remember the lives of the deceased. The celebratory dimension of the tradition means people are better equipped to support each other and it makes it easier for people to talk about. It's a great way of connecting people in grief with those who are not.' Put simply, death and grief do not have to be morbid.

I once asked a friend to join me in volunteering at a hospice over Christmas. She looked askance at me, before declining and saying, 'But everyone there is dying,' without even asking any more about it. It's a sad assumption that a person who is dying is someone to be feared and that it will be less enjoyable spending time with them than with someone who isn't. Frankly, I've found that those who are facing death often have a much better sense of humour than those who live life as though they are immortal. When I leave the hospice after a morning helping at the gym, I walk out bouncing with life and a feeling of softness that I don't experience in the same way any other day of the week.

Death is also something of a taboo in the States. Whereas before the civil war, most families would tend to the dead in their own homes, the law in some states now dictates that you have to hire a funeral home to care for your deceased. With the growing trend of big professional funeral homes in America, families don't realise that they can still look after their relative's body at home. So unless the funeral directors tell them it is their choice, most families unwillingly let their deceased loved ones be taken away and kept in funeral homes. If the dead are taken away like this, regardless of the preferences of the bereaved, the impact on them and the way they process their grief can be significant. This emphasis on the 'professional death' is just another way in which society adds to the taboo.

Of course, death is scary. As certain as it is, it is also an unknown; it is at once physical and yet invisible; and it is entirely out of our control. Indeed, psychologically speaking, death – or rather, our mortality – is the biggest evoker of existential crises in individuals. Dr Irvin Yalom, renowned American existential psychiatrist centred his writings on the four 'givens' of the human condition: isolation, meaninglessness, freedom and mortality. In other words, the scariest things about the nature of our lives are the fact that we're alone, that we are meant to have a purpose, that we're tied down by responsibilities and that we're all going to die. Of these four, death is the most frightening, so, understandably, people often choose to deny it. But just as the existentialists would say, taking action to overcome this fear is possible and very worthwhile. In doing so, we can live our lives with more depth, meaning and freedom than ever before.

Modern language with all its euphemisms and abbreviations is really very accommodating – encouraging, even – of a societal avoidance of death. This, in turn, creates a wedge between those who experience immediate loss and those who are on the periphery; as Iris Murdoch once wrote: 'The bereaved cannot communicate with the unbereaved.' Yet, as true as this is, it need not remain so – not if we don't want them to. This book is all about communication. It explores how the bereaved communicate their needs, and how people respond to them.

It's not just language that makes integrating death as an accepted part of life a challenge. In modern society death has almost become unnatural. Everything is geared towards youth. Employers can be ageist, and we've enlisted Botox, plastic surgery and anti-ageing creams and serums (. . . the list goes on) in our fight against the inevitable. And with every new cure for disease and preventative procedure we believe we are that little bit more indestructible – that we should live for ever. Death doesn't really fit into this kind of world.

Changing the Status Quo

Nevertheless, it seems that a relationship is beginning to evolve in favour of a greater understanding and acceptance of death. In 2009, photographer Walter Schels and his partner, journalist Beate Lakotta, curated an exhibition of photographs at the Wellcome Collection ('Life Before Death'), featuring hospice patients in the moments before and after their death. By looking death in the face, quite literally, touching it, watching it, capturing it, they claim to have been able to overcome their own fear of the dead and of being dead. If we could all do this, then surely we would also be better placed to comfort those who are left behind after someone has died.

In fact, this confrontation can be a wonderful, sociable thing. Take the recent Death Café movement as an example. Who would have thought that someone could make a social franchise out of talking about death? But Jon Underwood has done just that. London-based Underwood started Death Café in 2011, based on the ideas of Swiss sociologist and anthropologist Bernard Crettaz. Jon believed the best thing that he could do to help make this a better planet was to put an end to 'death denial'. Now, all over the world, strangers meet up in homes and cafés to talk about death and dying over coffee and cake. The rapid growth of Death Café is a clear reflection of the increasing number of people who want to participate in a dialogue around death. Something is in the air. It's time for death to take centre stage.

And what better way to facilitate this, than through the most powerful uniting phenomenon: the internet. Social media have provided a new and very different stage for us human beings to act out the drama of our lives – and deaths. People are now tweeting from their deathbeds; like the terminally ill Dr Kate Granger, who asked her Twitter followers for the best hash-tag for her dying moment. Suggestions included #onedieseveryminute, #deathbedlive and #finalcountdown. Not only this, but people can now create secret messages to be sent out posthumously via social networks. Dead Social, an organisation that calls itself a 'digital legacy tool', exists so that people can create a series of secret messages that are only released once they have died.

The response to these new online avenues suggests that there is a new hunger in humanity to engage with death and dying and to bring them into our daily lives, rather than keeping them locked up in the basement of our psyches.

So I hope this book can be seen as a gentle invitation to build a different relationship with death and grief. Changing our way of feeling and thinking about death is an opportunity to change our way of feeling and thinking about life, to deepen our lives and live them without fear. This means this book is not just for middle-aged and elderly people beginning to think about their own deaths. This is a book for all human beings. Death and grief are not discriminatory. If we can all start participating in this dialogue, then I am convinced we will not only find more meaning to life, but we will also be far better placed to support those who are left behind when someone they love has died.

I am fully aware I am not the first or only person to suggest this. Many great writers, bloggers, journalists have spoken with much more experience and far more poetically about this before: Meghan O'Rourke, Rachel Cook, Dannie Abse and Julian Barnes to name just a few. But we're still only at the beginning and, surely, the more the better? After all, we're never going to not die.

No One Size Fits All

While grief is the natural response to loss, it is still a personal thing, and people do it differently, depending on their upbringing, culture, who they are grieving for, how the person died and many other factors. There is no 'right' way of grieving and I am not claiming that the stories featured here reflect the universal reality of a bereaved mind. But I do hope that they give some kind of insight into what is helpful for a bereaved person, as well as what is not – because it is important to remain aware that what one person craves (a hug, for example) may be anathema to another; and even that what someone feels they need one day, might upset them the next. This is something that will become apparent as you read through the various stories, and while it might, on one level, make the job of 'the supporter' seem that much more difficult, an understanding and awareness of these conflicts and inconsistencies, along with your knowledge of the person you are supporting, should, ultimately, be helpful.

There is also much to be learned from the stories themselves, aside from the practical advice dispensed by the contributors. The differences that emerge should, hopefully, embolden you and give you the courage to identify your own friend or loved one's needs and to act accordingly. You may not always get it right, but don't shy away from trying.

There are moments in my story and those of the other contributors, which might seem brutal and harsh. Indeed, it was rather strange rereading what I wrote over two years ago, as I am, of course, in a very different place now. But that's not to say that what I was feeling then wasn't real, and I have to honour the grieving me at that time. Some contributors are talking several years after their bereavement, but they have all reflected as far as possible on what they felt in the initial stages of grief.

This is a book filled with personal experiences which are designed to open up a conversation. Neither I nor any of the other contributors is giving advice with the expectation that people should have known what to do, and should now always get it right. This is just a chance to express what it was like in the hope that talking and asking about death and grief become a little easier, more acceptable and more of a 'done thing'.

I have chosen to focus on two main themes – the lessons that we can learn from what people said to the bereaved and the actions they took in order to help them:

1. What can you say – and avoid saying?

Our voice resonates with life. Because this is so, it can touch the lives of others. The caring and compassion imbued in your voice finds passage to the listener's soul, striking his or her heart and causing it to sing out; the human voice summons something profound from deep within, and can even compel a person into action.

Daisaku Ikeda, President of the Sokka Gakkai

Personally speaking, words have been my saviour. If I hadn't found some solace in writing down and trying to articulate the mess of emotions that consumed me in the days, weeks and months after Mum died, I'm not sure I would have survived. Equally, some of the words – both written and spoken – from family and friends soothed me in ways that no amount of sleep, drink or food could. But words can be powerfully damaging too. This is what makes language so magical. My psychotherapy training has taught me a great deal about how we express ourselves most effectively, and the importance of learning to use words skilfully, with empathy and without expectation.

2. What helped – and what didn't?

Inaction breeds doubt and fear. Action breeds
confidence and courage. If you want to conquer fear, do
not sit home and think about it. Go out and get busy.
Dale Carnegie, American writer and lecturer

Doubt and fear also breed inaction, and being faced with supporting someone at such a vulnerable and painful time in their life might, understandably, evoke such emotions. But, just as Carnegie says, action – no matter how small it might be – can be enormously positive, creating confidence and courage in both the bereaved and the supporter.

Being present and available to our friends and loved ones is crucial at the best of times. In times of crisis it can be difficult to find our role in the support 'system', especially if there are seemingly plenty of other people around. But there are all sorts of ways we can make our presence known, which in itself might be the only thing the bereaved person needs.

These forms of support provide a point of reference throughout the book and a link between each story.

* * *

Every contributor was interviewed by me. I found them by word of mouth, and they vary in age, gender and background. Names and other identifying particulars have been changed. The individuals have nothing in common, except for their experience of bereavement – each has suffered what I would consider an 'immediate loss' – that of a parent, child, sibling, partner or best friend.

We begin with my own story.

Chapter 1

Annie, whose mother died

'She's gone, chicken.' Those were the words that told me my mum had died. It was 6.30 in the morning and two of my best friends were sleeping next to me.

The previous four days had been interminable, waiting for the inevitable, yet never really believing it would come. It was bizarrely warm and sunny for mid-October, so my dad, brother and I had just sat in the garden with whichever visitor was there, chain smoking and drinking endless cups of tea and coffee, as we waited for Mum to die. We would take turns going upstairs and moistening her mouth with the pink cotton buds – or lollipops, as Mum called them – talking to her and telling her what we were up to downstairs. She could barely talk or focus her eyes, but her spirit still sparkled. We observed helplessly as her body rapidly stopped functioning.

The night before she died, my brother Tommy, Dad and I went up to sit with her. She was feeling restless, so with great difficulty we helped sit her up – she was literally skin and bones, so the lightest touch was very painful. We told her that Dad had just cooked us spaghetti Bolognese and that it was actually rather good and she laughed and looked at him, mumbling, 'Not as good as mine though'. We all laughed, then cried, amazed that this miraculous woman, who was to die in fewer than twenty-four hours, could still crack a joke. Indeed, the night nurse on duty told us that only an hour before she died she had been demanding ice cream.

When I finally heard the dreaded words that I had been trying so hard to prepare for I jumped out of bed and paced the room repeating, 'Oh my God, oh my God'. My heart was pounding and my body would simply not stop moving. I remember time seemed to stop and I thought to myself, 'This is that moment; we're here. What am I feeling?' But I didn't really feel anything except the adrenaline pumping through me. It was like an out-of-body experience as I observed the first stages of grief.

My dad had been sleeping downstairs (my parents were no longer together and he had remarried) so I waited until he had got dressed and then we went into the bedroom together. I was terrified of looking at Mum, so I shielded my face with my hand. But I knew I had to look. Slowly, I let her face come into my line of vision. I was relieved she hadn't lost all her colour yet. It just looked like she was in a very deep and peaceful sleep. I walked over to her and forced myself to hold Mum's hand. Thankfully, it was still warm. I then let out a great wail.

The next few hours were like something out of a film. Everyone poured themselves something alcoholic and lit up cigarettes. Phones were ringing, lists were being written and I couldn't stop moving. I paced the garden as I went through my phone book telling everyone. I had this overwhelming need to pass on this new piece of information – I wanted the whole world to know and, for the first time, I wasn't afraid of telling people bad news. I felt that everyone needed to know that something extraordinary had happened – that a great human being who had played such a significant role in so many lives had just left the world. It was almost as though I wanted to hand out a slice of pain to everyone in a vain attempt at making it untrue, or more real, I'm not sure which – but I was certain that the less I had of it, the less of it I would have to carry.

People started arriving – cousins, aunties, uncles – and I welcomed it. I really wanted there to be life around me – hustle and bustle, activity, chatter, warmth. I guess it provided distraction. I didn't want anyone to leave, and to this day I wish they had been around more. I've always wanted a bigger family, but never more so than that day.

Visitors took turns going upstairs to see Mum and say goodbye for the final time, but I was finding it increasingly difficult to go into her bedroom because I couldn't bear to see her looking dead. I felt desperate to protect the last image I had of her alive.

When the undertakers arrived to take Mum away I panicked – partly because I didn't want her to go, knowing she'd never come back; but also because that meant I would have to go back into her room to get the dress we had chosen together three days earlier.

Mum had woken up and told us she thought she was going to die very soon. In panic, I started reeling off questions as they came into my head – things that I thought I might want to ask her in later years like, 'How will I know you're looking over me?' and 'What shall I call my children?', to which Mum replied they would tell me. Then we had set about choosing an outfit from her vast wardrobe for her funeral. We decided on a dress and shoes and she also told me what jewellery she wanted to wear and was happy to have cremated with her.

That first day after Mum died was extraordinarily special. All of my brother's friends and mine were there and we sat in the garden talking and laughing – great roaring laughter. I would never have believed anyone if they'd told me of the smiles and love that I would experience that day. I have never felt so held.

Towards the end of the day I started to get the 'waves': great sweeping rushes of agony that paralyse you for a moment and wash off you as quickly as they arrive. But with each one, I had my friends around me, breathing through the pain with me, crying with me. Strangely, I sometimes long for that day. I long for the warmth that came from being so surrounded and being so close to Mum's death. I long for that day when everyone was thinking about her.

If only every day could have been like that one. And for a while it wasn't far off. Some of my friends practically moved in – in fact, one of them did – but inevitably, over time, people started drifting. It was at this point, though, that the waves often seemed to drown me for a little while longer.

What Does It Feel Like?

It's a strange thing having time to prepare for loss. What on earth do you do with it? Constantly imagine life without the one who's dying? That's certainly what I tried to do. I was so aware of having this precious time that, sadly, many people do not get, that I wanted to use it wisely. I wanted to ensure that I would never look back and think, 'If only ... '

The truth is, you can't ever really prepare. Yes, you can get all the practicalities sorted, and discuss funeral preferences, all of which does, inevitably, make difficult decisions easier later on. But you don't really ever believe the person will die; and you certainly don't think it's true that once they have died, you can never ever see them again. So one way or another, the regrets do seep in eventually.

For me, the most important person in my life was now dead so, of course, the whole universe also had to cease to exist as it was at that moment. At least that's how Death Day felt to me: and everything did actually stop in my immediate world. Anything that resembled normality became unrecognisable. I couldn't relate to anyone whose life was about anything other than the fact that Mum had died. I even struggled to understand why strangers weren't coming over to me and saying how sad they were.

I am conscious of how odd this must sound, but I think it was really just a desperate attempt to find some meaning in what had just happened. It was about recognising that this wonderful woman wasn't alive any more. I think it came from a place of protectiveness, of Mum and her life – much like I'd imagine a parent feels for a child. I desperately wanted the memory of her life to be cherished by everyone. Of course, it was also, in part, a profound need for people to help soothe the pain of my loss. But it was also about acknowledging the fact that her life had been cut short.

No one ever knows how they will react when they lose someone they love, even if they have the time to prepare. My brother got busy making Bloody Marys for everyone. At the time, I couldn't imagine ever sleeping again. In fact, I feared going to sleep because I was so frightened of waking up and forgetting for one second what had happened and then having to experience the horror of my new reality all over again. My dad, a few days later, went round the house packing all her silver and jewellery and anything remotely valuable into a suitcase and drove it to his farm in Sussex to keep it all safe. In his state of shock, he just needed to do something immediately, and this was the first thing that came to mind.

A rather refreshing thing to come from the sense that life has paused was, for me, that you can only really live from moment to moment. I remember being very aware that I felt like I sometimes did when travelling, in that I could only function on instinct. I wasn't capable of really thinking about things: I just either did them or didn't. Sometimes I needed to be prompted to do things, like eating and sleeping, but in terms of what I did with the days that followed – going to the shops, watching a movie, which movie to watch – my senses were so heightened as to what was right and wrong for me that I was more decisive than I have ever been before or since.

That's not to say that every decision you make in this state is right – especially big ones – but in terms of day-to-day living, I felt totally in control. On the morning of Mum's funeral, I sent a text to my best friend asking her to pass on a message to everyone to *not* hug me. It was a totally visceral feeling – I knew I did not want to be flooded with hugs, that my personal breathing space should not be invaded that day.

Although my dad was wonderful when Mum died, it cannot be denied that had my parents been together things would have been very different for me. For a start, I most probably wouldn't have relied so heavily on my friends. As things stood, I did need my friends and the people around me to adapt to my rhythm, as much as they could. Some weren't working full-time and for them it was much easier to stop their normal routine, but even those who had to go to work every day made an effort to immerse themselves in the strange, but ultimately, rather lovely bubble of constant love and company that was created in my mum's house over the days and weeks that followed.

What Can You Say – and Avoid Saying?

On the whole, I liked talking about it, although not everybody does. For me, it helped to unravel this bizarre experience that had been imposed on my life.

My grandfather was particularly great at being openly inquisitive as to what my brother and I might be feeling. We went to visit him a few months after Mum died, at around the point people had begun to drift, and he effectively interviewed us. It was wonderful. He asked things like, 'What does it feel like to lose a mother so young?' and 'Was there a moment when you knew it was going to happen?' and 'What is your most prominent last image of her?' Of course, we spent most of the 'interview' crying, but when we got in the car to drive home we both breathed a huge sigh of relief – it was as though someone had just told us that the door to speak about Mum and this huge event we'd just experienced was still very much open, and that there were people on the other side of it with open arms waiting and ready to listen.

However, I also know now that I often expressed my grief vocally to serve the people around me. And this wasn't always such a positive thing. The control freak in me took it upon herself to ensure that everyone around me understood what I was feeling, so that they'd feel safe in my company – and also so they'd think I was dealing with it well. Explaining my grief to others meant I could pretend to myself that I was strong. I believed that if I talked about my feelings articulately and presented them neatly and accessibly, then people wouldn't worry about me and I could avoid feeling the feelings that would cause me to break down. The consequence of this was that over a year later I had a mountain of repressed and unaddressed raw grief that I had to actually 'feel'. That was ugly.

The safest bet with words is to be honest. If you don't know what to say, then say just that: 'I don't know what to say – this is awful.' It was the people who tried to make it OK that drove me mad, saying things like, 'You're being so strong.' You're allowed to not know how to deal with it, so don't feel you have to pretend; you'll probably find that as soon as you admit to being frightened of talking about it, you won't feel so frightened.

The sort of responses that felt sincere and appropriately weighty to me were along the lines of: 'I can't imagine what you must be feeling right now'; 'Your mum was such a fabulous woman'; 'I'm so sorry'; 'I'm thinking of you all'.

As for what not to say, in my experience verbal blunders often come when people don't think about or mean what they're saying. Words are powerful, so use them wisely. We all respond differently to different words, and we have different needs, depending on our experience of grief. What I tell you here won't be exactly the same as it is for everyone else in this book. But I'd say that on the whole, words said out of panic, fear or embarrassment are more likely to hurt. So take your time.

For me, things like, 'What can I do?' or 'Let me know if there's anything I can do' put me in a position where *I* would then have to think of something to offer the friend or relative in question. If there is something you actually want to do to help, then offer it specifically; say, 'I'll take the dog for a walk tomorrow' or 'I'm going to cook for you this weekend'.

'It will be OK' was another thing I didn't want to hear. For me, the one thing I knew for certain was that nothing would ever be OK again. More importantly, I didn't *want* it to be OK; the idea that life without Mum could be OK was not a comfort. What did that say about her and how important she was?

Conversely, I did take comfort in hearing from my peers who had lost a parent. I wanted to hear that they were still functioning and that this dreadful reality does not destroy you for ever. I rang a dear friend of mine who had lost her mother only two years before and she simply said, 'Annie, remember, if you want a packet of Twiglets, ask for Twiglets.' It was perfect to be given permission to ask for what I needed.

'Hope you're OK' – this was the most common statement of all, tagged on at the end of a text, email or Facebook message. While I know the intention was good, it always felt so thoughtless and dismissive. What's more, it doesn't invite any response from the bereaved person at all. What if they're not OK? Would you be able to handle it if you received a reply saying, 'I'm not OK, I feel like I can't breathe.' Think about what you're actually trying to say before you use this phrase. And then say that instead. If you're hoping they are surviving in the midst of the trauma, then say that. If you genuinely want to know what the bereaved person is feeling, ask them, 'How do you feel right now?'

It's not just what you say, it's how you say it too. Rados (or Radish as we called her), our bolshie Bulgarian cleaner who adored Mum, had me and my friends in much-needed hysterics after Mum died.

As it happens, she'd only found out about Mum when she saw her body being carried out of the house. The first thing she said when she saw me was, 'Annie, why you not tell me?' 'Oh I'm sorry Rados,' I said, 'we had quite a lot of people to tell this morning, it's been quite busy. 'Yes, but why you not make sure you tell me first ... I'm so upset Annie, I am going to miss her,' she said. Then she sat with her head in her hands saying, 'When you want me to come to work? ... You must make messy because at times like this, I have to work.'

What I remember most about this exchange is that I laughed – *a lot*. So much so that I wrote down what she had said straight away. It's interesting that it was my friends who were getting angry with her and wanting to take her away, and me that was rather enjoying her bluntness.

The point here is that only hours after Mum's death I was able to gauge whether or not someone was speaking authentically. I think what enabled me to feel at ease with such bluntness and seeming insensitivity is that Rados was just so real – she was being herself, and treating me like myself too. It seems to me that so many of the blunders from family and friends came from an assumption that someone who's just hours into their grieving somehow stops being the person they were – that they turn into a fragile flower that needs to be tiptoed around. So while Rados's manner could be considered brutal, I think I actually took pleasure in her speaking so candidly.

What Helped – and What Didn't?

As I said earlier, if you want to do something to help, don't ask for a job – either offer one or just do it: go shopping, cook dinner, vacuum the floor, take the dog out. They may seem like trivial tasks, but they are crucial in enabling life to go on, and provide you with an easy way to get stuck in.

Small things like responding to text messages can also make a big difference. I had been seeing a boy for a few months before my mum died and we called it off because I wanted to focus on her. He had promised to be a great friend through my impending trauma, so two days after Mum died I called on his support: I sent him a text telling him my friends were coming round for a little booze-up and that I would love for him to be there. Over twenty-four hours later I still hadn't heard from him. I eventually got a text from him saying he'd been busy at work and he'd call me later. When he eventually did, he told me the real reason he hadn't replied was that he wasn't sure I was dealing with things very well so he'd thought it best not to reply.

A response of silence when I'd reached out was incredibly hurtful. I think that no matter what *you* might think is the 'right' way of dealing with things, always respond in some way or another and be wary of imposing your views.

My friends established a rota through email, so they knew that someone was always with me for the night in the days and weeks after Mum died. Bar a few moments when I chose to go for a walk, I wasn't alone for a second for the first three weeks and it was amazing. My bathroom was filled with various friends' toothbrushes and different people's pyjamas were strewn about my bedroom. Each day the friend 'on duty' would bring a new batch of DVDs and a supply of scented candles (I became very sensitive to smell). All I had to do was open the door, return to the sofa and leave them to it. They cooked delicious meals and they'd chat away to me and to each other, even if I was lying comatose in the other room. In fact, my most comforting moments were when I was lying on the sofa on my own, listening to the hubbub in the kitchen as my friends talked among themselves. I just loved that they were looking after themselves, seemingly unworried about me – although, of course, I knew they were.

This level of busyness and company might not be for everyone, but for me it was perfect. So most importantly, I think, don't assume the person wants to be alone or that they have enough people around them. Ask them, or wait for them to tell you to bugger off.

Staying in touch is important too. I distinctly remember taking enormous comfort in every text I received in the days that followed mum's death. Of course, this might not apply to everyone, particularly those of an older generation, but nevertheless it is a simple way to express your care. My phone never left my hand and every text felt like a new blanket of support being wrapped around me – with every acknowledgement, my wounds were licked a little more. I was almost disappointed when there was no one left to tell because I wouldn't receive any more texts. Knowing that people knew was the first step in feeling supported. So I would say that regardless of how well you know the person who's left behind, always acknowledge it – it can't do any harm, and although it may be hard to believe, it might do an awful lot of good. I still remember hearing from people I barely knew and really cherishing the messages they sent; it meant that even if for only a few seconds, they had thought about my mum and the loss of her life. And one thing is certain – the ones who stay silent stand out. As Martin Luther King put it: 'We will remember not the words of our enemies, but the silence of our friends.'

Funerals can be awkward, and that's when the fear of approaching the bereaved kicks into gear big-time. It was uncomfortable when I saw people there, at the wake, in my house, who obviously knew who I was, but who chose not to come over and say hello. I understand that it may have been with the best intentions – not wanting to bombard me, or a fear of what to say – but I think there is more risk in ignoring than in making an approach. A very old friend of my mum's made a point of waving at me as I walked down the aisle behind Mum's coffin. It took me several moments to register that this person was deliberately waving at me, trying to get my attention, but once I did, he nodded and smiled, clearly just letting me know he was there. It was an extraordinarily comforting moment and, as a result, even though it was a long time before I saw him again, I will always remember his presence around that time.

In simply acknowledging the death, you enter into the bereaved person's world. I found it astonishing the number of people that just ignored the catastrophe that had recently occurred in my life. The problem with not acknowledging it, especially so early on, is that it puts the bereaved person on mute. They no longer have the opportunity or permission to be sad if they need to be, or talk about it, because the people around them haven't opened up a space for it. And in those early days, it's incredibly hard to carve out that space yourself. When I've asked people since why they didn't mention it, they've mostly said something along the lines of, 'Well, I didn't want to bring it up', as though I might have forgotten my mum had died. If someone said simply, 'I'm so sorry Annie', or even gave me a knowing look and squeeze of the arm, it was not likely to send me crumbling to the floor in tears in the middle of a drinks party (after all, I had geared myself up to face the music, have small talk, and smile), but I still wanted the facts of my life at that moment to be recognised. The energy and effort required in order to cope when people are ignoring your situation is utterly isolating and, in many ways, it made me feel more in touch with my pain than if people had said a few words in acknowledgement.

Having said that, I'd be lying if I didn't admit that there were times when I was caught off guard and broke down in public, seemingly out of the blue. And yes, sometimes it might have been because of something someone said. Nevertheless, I remain an advocate of acknowledging no matter what. What's so bad about public displays of distress, anyway? Our discomfort in dealing with crying comes from fear and a need to fix. Many people feel afraid of vulnerability. But giving someone space to express that tender powerlessness, simultaneously encourages them to bring forth their strength and courage ... a deeper much truer power.

It's important to be constant, and not disappear over time. When the weeks turn to months, and for friends, life really does go back to normal, people start to slip away. But the person left behind needs the support just as much then, if not more than before. This is when texts come in really handy. One friend texted me pretty much every day for the first four months after Mum died. I didn't see her particularly often, but she was much more present in my experience of grief than those friends I heard from infrequently, but who would then want to take me out for dinner and ask what it had been like for the last few weeks. If you're not there from the beginning, you'll miss the boat, and when it next comes around, it'll be unrecognisable.

Also, make sure you remember the important milestones – the first month, the first time your friend comes home from holiday, the first new experience they have that they can't share with their lost loved one. There will be countless firsts and all of them significant, even if it's over a year later.

And lastly …

Be prepared for the long haul. Only the person who has just lost someone they love knows at that moment that life will never be the same again. I remember nudging one very dear friend who went off the radar about two months after Mum died and he replied saying, 'Annie, people's lives get busy, you know'. I was so hurt by this – not because his life was busy, but because it felt to me that there was some kind of expectation for me to remember this. I couldn't comprehend any life outside of my grief, let alone a busy one, and here I was being told that there were people who weren't thinking about the fact my mum was dead *all* the time. Three years on, I reflect on this and think, 'Christ – what a nightmare I must have been', but the truth is, it's only now that I have got to grips with the fact that life goes on, with or without Mum. So to hear this after only two months was incomprehensible. Of course, people's lives move on, and of course, they move on much, much faster than that of the bereaved person, but I guess the thing to do is at least to *pretend* you're still there alongside them … because the slightest thing is going to make them feel utterly alone in the world.

Grief is not an event, it is a process, and processes don't have a finishing line. So be prepared for this. It will give you an opportunity to lodge a reminder in your subconscious to check in every now and then and allow for the fact that they might not be OK, even when it's been over a year and things are seemingly 'back to normal'.

Chapter 2

Molly, whose husband died

My husband, Felix, passed away, aged fifty, on 17 December 2012, just after our tenth wedding anniversary, following a two-and-a-half-year battle with prostate cancer.

I met Felix in 1994 when I was twenty-eight, at an evening class in ballroom dancing. A year later he moved in and we got married in 2002 in Spain. Eight years later Felix started getting pains in his right knee, and after a few tests and scans we were informed that he had advanced prostate cancer, and that even though he was only forty-seven (the average age for people to die from prostate cancer is seventy-two), his illness was terminal: nothing could be done. We asked about life expectancy and were told, 'Not too long, so you should get your financial affairs sorted.'

I broke down. We'd had a terrible journey already, getting to the point of diagnosis, with delayed scan results, missing notes and general incompetence. It got so bad that we nearly moved to my native Spain. Hearing the news was like being run over by a freight train. I – we – could not imagine that Felix was so ill. He'd had no symptoms other than the pain in his knee. He hadn't even had any blood in his urine (often a key sign) until the day of the diagnosis.

There followed another rollercoaster ride around healthcare in both the UK and Spain, but we eventually managed to get Felix on an even keel, so that he was able to enjoy a good quality of life until more or less the last three months of his life.

Although neither of us really believed he was going to die from his illness, we spoke very openly about all possibilities and had many painful conversations, some of which I tape-recorded and still listen to. His first rule was that I was not to keep anything from him. So we discussed everything. We read all we could find about prostate cancer, and he kept a journal. I think because of this I never lost hope that he would survive. I thought: if anyone can beat this, he can.

Felix's family and friends were respectful and supportive of our way of dealing with things. His best friend, Peter, was away a lot, but came round as soon as he heard of the illness. He agreed with me and said if anyone could beat it, it would be Felix. My brother, on the other hand, was brutally matter-of-fact, saying, 'He's not going to come out of this'. Of course, now I understand that he was being realistic, but I reacted badly at the time.

Felix passed away peacefully in his sleep at a hospice. I was told that he had lasted longer than expected and I put that down to the fact that he had a high pain threshold and that he had not wanted to leave me alone. I was with Felix's brother, Richard, who had come to the hospice to be with me. We stayed with Felix, kissing him, hugging him, talking to him, while his body was still warm, and then we left to go home.

What Does It Feel Like?

I was surprised by my immediate reaction. I thought I would feel desperate and beside myself, but the day that Felix passed away,

I was very calm. I was so calm, in fact, that I remember driving all the way home from the hospice without shedding a tear. I was, despite my loss, totally in control.

After that I cried now and then, but not in a distraught, violent manner – no wailing. I just cried quietly. I suppose that I was so exhausted by the whole experience of watching someone I love die, that by the time of his death I had no strength left. I felt like I was drifting effortlessly on a cloud, with no energy, just very light.

I functioned well in the weeks that followed. This was probably partly due to the pressure of knowing I needed to return our Motability car within a few weeks, and wanting to get as much done as possible while I still had it. This helped me to stay focused on practical things, like taking Felix's clothes to the charity shops and donating all his medicines to Inter Care. Had it not been for this pressure, I'm sure I wouldn't have done anything and all his things would still be around the house. Even now I find it hard to get things done.

I did all of this on my own, which was fine. It wasn't out of choice, but I simply didn't have anyone around to help me. My brother-in-law had gone back to Wales and I didn't want to go with him. And as it was Christmas, everyone else was away.

What Can You Say – and Avoid Saying?

I found some reactions to the news of Felix's death quite difficult to deal with because so many people were expecting it, and I wasn't. I sent a text to one friend just saying her name. She knew what I was telling her and her response was, 'Already?' I couldn't believe she had even considered him dying. Another friend just said, 'Hmmm', again, as though it was totally expected. People would say to me, 'But he was so ill, Molly', but I had clearly been in denial. I was completely shocked and found it unsettling to think they'd all seen something I hadn't.

I keep thinking that I haven't seen Felix in over a year, and the thought that if I live for another twenty years, I will not see him for this long is overwhelming. It really hurts. I miss him more now than I did in the months immediately after his death, so when people say to me that time will heal, it does sometimes annoy me. I know it's said out of kindness, and I just accept it, but each day that I live a new experience that Felix is not there for, it hurts. I had a stinking cold a few weeks ago and was feeling down, thinking of Felix and what he would have done to cheer me up. I thought of how he would have prepared some tomato soup and a hot toddy and would have looked after me. If these moments are acknowledged then perhaps some of the pain might be eased.

A lot of people say, 'I can imagine how you must be feeling', which is also annoying. Of course, I do realise that they are well-meaning, and it is generally said in an honest (if sometimes clumsy) attempt at trying to give comfort. (At least they've said something!) But sometimes it actually feels quite hurtful.

A neighbour once said to me, 'Life is hard, isn't it?' There was no, 'I am sorry for your loss' – just a simple statement that life is hard. She was also a widow, so I think it was an awkward attempt at empathy. But I was so shocked I had no idea how to respond.

The words I found the hardest were when people asked me how I was. The question would elicit one (or more) of three responses:

1. I would burst into tears.
2. I would lie, stating that I was fine when I was not.

3. I would completely deflect the question and ask the other person how he/she was to divert the attention away from myself.

I know it is normal and kind to ask how someone feels, but coming from close friends, who really know how you feel by simply looking in your eyes, this question can put you under a lot of pressure to appear OK, and this isn't helpful.

The best thing is to give the bereaved person a hug and tell them, 'You will be all right'. Of course, there are many times when this doesn't feel comforting, as the last thing you want to think is that you will be OK without the person you have lost. But, it's all in the delivery: when people I know – and who know me well – tell me with sincerity and tenderness that I'll be OK, that's reassuring, and I find it less pressurising than being asked how I am.

I found that some people communicate better in writing. Some friends I'm not very close to wrote statements like, 'Things will get better', which feels really meaningless, but my closest friends wrote really beautiful words, and when they wrote about Felix and me, it brought me enormous strength. Felix's best friend, Peter, sent me an email on the first anniversary of Felix s death, telling me how he was laughing to himself, remembering times with Felix on a flight back from New York. He also told me that I have earned my place in heaven for having looked after Felix the way I did during his illness. I know that he meant every single word of it, and it was just so nice to be acknowledged.

It was also nice when people told me that they had learned a lot from the way Felix dealt with his illness – the sheer dignity that he showed and his strength. Our nephew told me that whenever he has a thumping headache, he says to himself: 'Think of Felix; don't be a wimp and carry on!'

In general, I feel very fortunate to have the friends that I have, as most of them have been there for me, but I realise that life goes on for them, so I have tended to shy away from them a little bit, so as not to burden them. Instead, I go to a weekly chat on death and dying at the hospice, which I find brilliant. I have stopped talking about these meetings to my friends because some of them suggested I might be dwelling on death too much. Obviously, I am aware that they are trying to protect me, and that they think that if I stop dealing with the hospice my pain will be less. But it's sad that their own fear of talking about death means I have to keep it from them. It creates more of a distance between us.

Perhaps the most memorable words came from a very wise, elderly lady who told me that 'life mistreats those who allow themselves to be mistreated'. She actually said this when Felix was still alive, so it made me persevere and look for more answers; it stopped me giving up on him. But since then, this statement has given me comfort because it reminds me I can have a say in what life does to me and how to respond to it. I've drawn enormous amounts of strength and calm from this. It has given me power.

What Helped – and What Didn't?

The best thing anyone could do for me was give me hugs and kisses. I am by nature a very demonstrative person and in my relationship with Felix there was a lot of physical affection, so I miss that desperately.

I think it may be a cultural thing because in Spain people hug all the time, whereas in the UK they seem to be less openly affectionate. I had got used to only kissing or hugging if I saw that the person in front of me wanted it, but after Felix died I often felt frustrated if a person was unable to hug me in a situation where it felt like that was the only thing that would comfort me. A close friend tried to explain that many people feel it is an invasion of personal space, but I was stunned. Surely the one thing we need more of in this world is human contact.

Fortunately though, most of my close friends felt very comfortable hugging me if I was crying, and many of them cried with me, which I appreciated. Ironically, my mother is not like me when it comes to hugging. I remember once when I was very upset, crying my eyes out, my mother entered the room and just stood there, looking at me. I said, 'Oh my God, you are an ice cube!' She apologised saying that it was not something that came naturally to her. I found this unbearable, but I have to accept it.

One close friend finds it difficult to respond when I am upset, so to avoid feeling bad I have tried not to cry in front of her. This means I have had to avoid her a lot of the time, which is exhausting. But she has been incredibly supportive in her own way and I've learned how best to call on her support. When Felix was in hospital, he would tell me to go home, open some wine and call her. So I would pick up the phone with a thumping headache, have a conversation and a laugh with her, and would put the phone down headache-free. She came to the UK and stayed with us before Felix died and she's always there for me now on the other end of the phone.

Regular contact with people has been very important. I have friends all over the world, and many old friends in Madrid. We speak every weekend on Skype or WhatsApp, and I know I can contact them whenever I want to without them feeling I am breathing down their necks.

I could never ask for company though, so I have only had people around me when they wanted to be there. And that is fine. I prefer it, in fact, as I'd worry that people come just for my sake – because they think I need them – rather than because they want to be there.

The fact that people make time for you is priceless. My friends all work full-time and are away a lot, so I know I can't expect to see them very often, but just knowing I have many friends I can call, and who will listen and talk to me, is all I need; they make time for me and that is what's important.

My siblings are also there for me in their own way. They make light-hearted comments to try to make me feel better. That's what my family does – we make jokes, but I know they're trying to ease my pain. They came over for a week after Felix died and that was brilliant. We spent every afternoon together and had a really good time. I loved being just the four of us, no partners – just us, drinking and eating and talking. They couldn't come to the funeral as they had to go back to Spain, but I understood and was grateful for that time we had together.

Felix's funeral was – like him – very beautiful and un-assuming, and I know he would have said to me, 'Molly, you got it spot on!' I met the priest a few days before to arrange the service and was dreading having to talk about Felix. But that morning, I received a lovely letter from a close friend of his, telling me stories of things that Felix had done as a child and what he was like as a friend. I thought that it was a perfect reflection of Felix's life, so I gave the priest a copy of the letter and he used it for the funeral service. Afterwards, people came up to me asking me if the priest had indeed known Felix.

After the funeral and cremation, a few family members and friends returned to our house and there was a kind of wake – a custom that was completely alien to me, but which was nice

nevertheless, arranged on the spur of the moment by my sister-
and brothers-in-law. At one o'clock we went to the local pub as
friends around the world had arranged to have a pint of
Guinness at that time. It was a lovely thought, and it humbled
me that people across the globe would be drinking Felix's
beloved beer all at the same time in his memory. I still find tears
rolling down my face thinking of this.

The most valuable source of support has come through the
hospice, as that is where I met Lyn. She is also Spanish, and her
husband passed away two weeks before Felix. I can be completely honest with her about my feelings and I can cry openly
without shame. I totally identify with her pain and her loss and
since we first met at the hospice, we've been getting together regularly for coffees and chats. I think finding someone who is
experiencing exactly the same pain and who is going through it
at the same time is enormously helpful so if you are able to help
the bereaved connect with such a person then you'll be a godsend.

The best gesture anyone made came from Felix's sister,
Elizabeth. When Felix's grandmother in Swansea passed away,
her piano was given to Elizabeth, and followed her to Germany
when she moved there a few years ago. Elizabeth knew that I
had told Felix I wanted to learn to play the piano and that he
had given me a keyboard which, to my great shame, I never
used when he was alive (something I will regret for the rest of
my life). So some time after Felix died Elizabeth not only offered
me the piano, but had it sent over from Germany. I know that
wherever Felix is, he will be over the moon that I am now learning to play on his grandmother's beautiful piano. It was a
fantastic and incredibly meaningful present.

And Lastly ...

Ultimately, I think 'being there' is about giving the person absolute confidence that whenever they need to they can pick up the phone and speak to you and that you will be happy to listen. And if you decide to pay a visit and give them a hug, then so much the better!

What you can learn from Molly's story

There are a few key lessons I think we can take from Molly's experience. The first being not to assume the bereaved will be expecting the death, even if the person died from a terminal illness. As I mentioned in my chapter, while someone may know intellectually that their loved one is going to die, hope always overpowers the mind. So be careful with what you say in reference to the inevitability of the death. It may be that the bereaved person needs to go through a process of talking as though it might not have happened, before they can come to accept their experience.

Also, take responsibility for your unique capacity as a supporter. If you absolutely know you are not able to be available for your friend in a particular way, for example dealing with tears, then let them know at the beginning and make up for it in some other way – find your own 'channel' of care.

Finally, don't be afraid to impose your presence and reassure your friend or loved one that you want to be there. Molly was very concerned that people were visiting out of duty, and this meant she often kept herself isolated. Tell them that you are with them because you sincerely want to be there, and share the burden of their experience.

Chapter 3

Beatrice, whose sister died

Margaret died when she was sixty-six. She was my only sister, and fourteen years my senior. By the time I'd left home and started university she was married with three children and living in a huge house. I remember going to visit her and thinking she seemed to have so much of everything.

Her marriage broke up though, and eventually she met someone else. She had been with her second partner for a long time when he left her for another woman. I'd never seen Margaret so devastated and it took her the best part of that year to get over it. I invited her to come on holiday with me. It was her sixty-fifth birthday and, for the first time ever, I treated my big sister to something. I will forever be grateful for that holiday – it was the sisters' experience I'd always dreamed of.

Days after we got back from holiday Margaret went on a work trip to Australia. One morning she didn't turn up to work and nobody could get hold of her. Eventually, her colleagues got the estate agent to break in to her house and she was found unconscious in bed. She'd had a major aneurism. Before I even knew anything about it Margaret had been rushed to hospital for emergency surgery to drain the blood from her brain. I got a call from my niece at 4 a.m. She said, 'Mum's had a terrible accident and is on life support.' I don't remember much of what I felt then. I think I was traumatised. It seemed that in that moment, the bottom had fallen out of my world. All I knew was that I had to get there.

It was at the airport that the hysteria began. I started sobbing at check-in and I don't think I stopped until I got to Sydney. I think being alone in the chaos of the airport was overwhelming and terrifying. I remember ringing a friend and saying, 'I don't know what I'm doing, but I'm about to board a flight to Sydney to see Margaret in hospital.' She told me to keep breathing and take a good sedative. The airport staff obliged by taking me to a prayer room where they gave me a Valium.

When I got to the hospital I saw Margaret's son who I hadn't seen for about five years. He looked terrible. We went to the ICU together, and there she was: hooked up to countless machines bleeping like sirens and with an enormous gash, clamped together with giant staples, across her forehead, all the way back to behind her ears. It was utterly shocking. And as I looked at her I just knew there was no way someone could go through that trauma and come back the same person. I knew right then that it was curtains for Margaret.

My nieces arrived the next day and then the wailing and the hysterics really kicked in. I remember feeling I needed to be the strong one, and I tried to hold it together. We saw the surgeon in a private room and he told us it was an incredibly serious situation: Margaret would never recognise anyone again, never be able to walk again and she'd have to be in intensive care for two or three years in Australia. The choice was either to turn the machine off and she might live for a week, maybe a month, or keep it on and ... who knows. There was nothing to consider, as far as I was concerned. I wanted to turn everything off, and I'd expect someone to do that for me; but the kids just couldn't comprehend it, and hoped there might be some other option. Twenty-four hours later though we all agreed and they turned the machines off immediately. Even at that point I think Margaret's children were still hoping she'd survive. But I knew there was no chance. There was just a body there, no life, no soul – her spirit had gone.

Once they'd unplugged Margaret, they cleaned her up a bit and she didn't look quite so bad. She died at 8.45 the following morning, quite peacefully. I've still got the nappy pin they used to wrap a towel around her head, and wear it on a chain around my neck.

What Does It Feel Like?

That night we all moved in to Margaret's house to embark on the post-death admin. That was horrendous. Being surrounded by her things in the place where she'd last been the Margaret I remembered – the cups she'd drunk from, the pillow she'd slept on – I began to experience short painful bursts of reality. I remember the girls and I were fighting over her handbag, each of us wanting to discover it precisely as it had been left, last touched by her – desperate attempts to connect with her as a living, breathing being.

While we were in the house I became obsessed with the fact that I couldn't find her blood pressure pills anywhere. Margaret and I had always had bad migraines and we both took the same medication to help manage them. She particularly needed them as she travelled so much. I looked everywhere, but I couldn't find them. I began thinking, If she'd had them, this wouldn't have happened ... What if ... If only ... I started thinking she must have stopped taking them deliberately. Maybe she wanted to end things because of the break-up with her partner. Maybe she'd given up. I couldn't help but think some part of her wanted this to happen. A part of me still believes that today.

Losing Margaret felt very different to my past experiences of grief. This time, I went into total meltdown and plunged myself into a cocoon for safety. I needed to be surrounded by familiar and comforting things: my cats, my flat, photographs, wine, soft things and, of course, friends.

I had no idea how to react. I didn't know what to do with Margaret's death. It was so sudden and unexpected, I was completely lost. What's more, I had to share my grief with my nieces and nephew and Margaret's grandchildren, and felt a responsibility to help them understand their loss too. Perhaps it made me need my own friends even more – I desperately wanted to be with people who allowed Margaret's death to be entirely about the loss of my sister. But I was too dazed and confused to know how to ask for help in any coherent way.

I couldn't listen to music for a very long time afterwards, as the noise felt like such an imposition. Light, sunshine, anything bright – it all felt meaningless. I wanted darkness and rain and for everything to be bad.

Margaret had been such a life force with such a powerful presence and I'm certain this affected the way I dealt with her death. I felt I'd lost my own identity somehow. I felt completely alone. I lost track of who I was because I didn't seem important any more. I quite often felt incredibly irrelevant. Why her and not me? I don't have kids, grandchildren ... It seemed so cruel for her to have been taken and not her younger, now empty and heavy-hearted sister.

My grieving process was tainted by the fact that I was made executor of the will. Tensions built dramatically within the family and I became vilified. They didn't trust me to get the job done and at times things got incredibly nasty between us all. The isolation I felt being Margaret's only sister was compounded by the fact that the rest of the family, to whom I should have been getting closer, viewed me as the enemy, which was terribly hurtful. This will always be with me, I think, and friends became an even more important resource to me as a consequence.

What Can You Say – And Avoid Saying?

It was very important to me to call a death a death. Call it by its real name. I became rather brutal about life and death and found it refreshing to have that mirrored back.

Voices were also very important; familiar voices from the past that jolted me into some kind of normality. It was so comforting to hear from people I grew up with who didn't know Margaret, but who just wanted to check in, tell me something mundane. Knowing that they were thinking of me meant a lot.

The best letters and conversations were those about Margaret and how she'd felt about me. One person wrote: 'I could tell how much she loved you and relied on you.' That brought me enormous amounts of strength.

My best friend's sister wrote to me and said, 'I love being a sister and am very happy to be here as a stand-in'. On reflection, I'm surprised this went down so well, but I think because I knew it was so sincere it was very comforting. I also valued that she didn't try and avoid the fact that she still had a sister. So many other people went to embarrassing lengths to pretend they didn't.

What didn't go down well was when people tried to make Margaret being dead somehow OK. Many people seemed not to know how to express their sorrow and compassion, and so instead they tried to make it better. Actually, I just wanted people to wallow with me, especially at the beginning, rather than tell me, 'She is in a better place' or, 'At least she didn't know what was happening to her'. I mean, what was I meant to say to that?

The God thing is tricky too. I'm not particularly religious, but I believe in something. God seemed to check out though, and while the idea that a kind of spirit lives on was some consolation, the idea of Margaret being in a 'better' place was just irritating. I wanted her to be in my place. I wanted her to comfort me in my grief, but that was the one thing I couldn't have.

Choosing when to say something face to face, or to write it is also worth thinking about. Some things just don't work in a letter, especially jokes. A distant friend who was so clearly trying to attempt humour with the best intention, wrote, 'You said she was looking great when you went on holiday, so at least she went out in style'. Somehow, in writing, this just didn't work – it left me cold, even though I know if I'd heard her say the same thing it wouldn't have felt so crass.

What Helped – and What Didn't?

I found it very useful having people around me. It was more about being around activity, rather than people doing anything specific for me. There's something about seeing people doing physical things, like cooking or cleaning, that assures you they aren't feeling embarrassed around death – that they can go about normal life in your presence.

I went to my doctor soon after I got back from Australia, as I knew I wasn't coping well. She prescribed anti-depressants, which helped, and suggested bereavement counselling which was amazing once I found the right person to talk to. The great thing about it was there were no expectations of how I should behave. I could go in and lie prostrate on the sofa one week, and bounce around telling jokes the next.

The funeral was very cathartic. It gave me a focus and occupied me when I most needed a diversion. Margaret had so many friends and supporters who rallied round, made food, arranged flowers and really helped us through the funeral arrangements and afterwards. People travelled from all over the world to be there, so there was a combined feeling of effort, love and sadness for a life cut short, but truly lived to the full.

I was so grateful to the friends who wanted to speak at her funeral – such a generous act. One friend spoke so beautifully about Margaret, which I will never forget: 'She shone her special light on the world and how she saw it. Turned it into a kaleidoscope of images and colours, found secret things and shared them with us. She saw things differently. She was precise and careful with her crafting of life. She knew about love and showed it in abundance. Like the bright light she was, she will not be extinguished.'

It was important to keep the distractions going after the funeral. I took a month off work and friends invited me away, not minding how I was or what I looked like, so I didn't feel I had to pretend. I really enjoyed meeting new people and being with strangers. Often, the reaction from strangers on hearing of my loss was so much more visceral and raw, and that was a great consolation. They also can't hurt you so easily, so I felt less anxious about how they would react to me. I had experienced such animosity from family that I found strangers refreshing. I could dance one minute and then sob the next and no one would judge me. Also, a lot of my friends had no experience of death at all, so I was drawn to people who had been bereaved before and that was sometimes someone new.

The regularity of contact also felt more important than the things people actually did. One cousin was great – she rang at the same time every day for weeks. I didn't need her to be with me, just her phone call every day was enough. Hearing about world tragedies also brought me some respite. I know it sounds awful, but hearing about a new civil war or another natural disaster helped me to put my own experience into perspective – just remembering that other people's lives are more tragic.

I became very close with one of Margaret's friends . . . lose a sister and gain a friend. I was drawn to her sense of humour and of reality: no bullshit. And she loved Margaret very deeply. We could share our love for her without competing over our relationship with her or our respective sense of loss.

I found commercial sympathy cards rather nauseating. Reading somebody else's sentiment over and over again just sort of numbs you. Letters, even Post-it notes were gratefully received – especially hand-made cards, but 'Sympathy' (or, very occasionally, 'Heartfelt Sympathy') becomes so meaningless when you see it printed across a card time and time again.

One needs to feel cherished, but it doesn't have to be through words. It's more about physical presence – warmth and being there, regardless of whatever state you're in, people taking you as they find you. Before leaving Australia, I became obsessed with getting Margaret's body back to the UK for the funeral. I really didn't want her to travel alone. The idea of us having to travel separately was so unbearable. I desperately wanted her to be on the same plane as me. It wasn't possible, but I remember how important it was to me to feel I had support when making those desperate attempts; that even if everyone around me was thinking, 'It's not possible; let it go, Beatrice', they were able to let me get to that point on my own – to go alongside me as I figured it out.

The Christmas after Margaret died I accepted an invitation from two of my closest friends to go with them to Spain. Unfortunately, it ended up being an exceptionally bad idea for all concerned. I completely lost it. I just couldn't believe there was anything more important than the fact that Margaret had died, and needed everything to be about that. I made a big scene and lost two of my closest friends for a long time. Of course, now I can reflect back and see how difficult I must have been, but at the time I couldn't function like a normal adult; I guess I needed people to be OK with that. It was a clear reflection of people who hadn't experienced loss before; they sort of thought it would go away, and they clung on to every moment I smiled, hoping I was better for ever. I probably behaved much worse because I wasn't being heard. The truth is, I wanted them to take responsibility for me and assure me I had the space to grieve in their presence, and at my own pace. I know now this meant accommodating difficult behaviour but it's not like it lasts forever.

I think if you've experienced it before, then you understand the unpredictable nature of grief: that you might feel like partying one minute, but then as soon as you start dancing you say, 'Oh no, sorry; didn't mean that. Put me back in the dark room please.' That needs to be allowed.

Although I lost some friends after Margaret died, bridges have been built, and over time you forget the carelessness and remember that so many people find grief and death hard to understand.

And Lastly . . .

The times I felt most enveloped with love and understanding were when I was home, with my home comforts. Never let someone in mourning feel lonely; make them laugh, if at all possible – humour is so important and too easily forgotten. Engage them with stories or diverting entertainment and feed them delicious food and drink to take away some of the pain. Being indulged really helps – feeling that anything and everything goes.

What you can learn from Beatrice's story

Beatrice's enthusiasm for counselling gives us a clue as to what a bereaved person might be looking for from their friends. She liked that she wasn't expected to behave in a particular way and further, that she wasn't expected to behave in the same way each week. Follow suit with your expectations: get your flexibility hat on and go with the flow.

Sometimes things that don't make sense or are obviously impossible will not be apparent to the bereaved. Beatrice couldn't bear the idea of her sister's body 'being alone'. Be patient in these moments – you don't need to launch into an explanation of the logic of the situation (for example, explaining that it's OK for the person to be alone because they're dead). Let them come round to the reality of the situation in their own time.

Finally, I think Beatrice's story demonstrates that sometimes, no matter how mature or grown up the bereaved person is, grief makes people feel beside themselves and therefore apt to throw a wobbly more easily and perhaps more frequently. Be compassionate.

Chapter 4

John, whose partner died

His name was Robert. We met when I was thirty-five, on 10 April 2004 after chatting online for some time. The connection was instantaneous and the friendship went from strength to strength. Very soon we were a couple.

During the process of buying our home together in June 2005, Robert developed a persistent cough. The doctors initially dismissed it as some kind of infection, and sent him away with antibiotics. But as soon as he'd finished them, he was back at the doctor's again, complaining of the same problem. This went on for several months. We assumed they knew best and had ensured that everything was being checked out properly, but in early September 2005 Robert woke up looking like a chipmunk, with a puffy left cheek. A biopsy was taken and a week later, when we were in the supermarket, we got a call telling us Robert had non-Hodgkin's lymphoma (a blood cancer varying in severity). We were both unfamiliar with this name, and assumed it must be relatively manageable. It wasn't until we went home and looked it up that the reality hit us. Suddenly everything felt heavy, and very frightening. I'd lost a grandmother to cancer, so it immediately triggered fears about what it could mean.

The doctors told us it was serious, but that there was about 60/40 chance of survival. Our hearts clung on to that 60 per cent. As frightening as this news had suddenly become, we knew we had an incredibly strong love for each other and we believed that could conquer anything.

Chemotherapy began in October 2005 but not long after, Robert was forced to stay in hospital because his body was reacting so violently to it. By December, Robert lay in his bed barely conscious and wracked with pain. A doctor advised me that chemo was no longer an option, as any more would most surely kill him.

The next two years were filled with highs and lows; periods of recovery, followed by repeat visits to hospital in agonising pain. I was no longer just Robert's partner, I was also his carer. I was living for two people and the responsibility was, at times, hard to bear. The diminishing intimacy between us also made things harder. Not only were we unable to make love any more, we didn't dare share our thoughts and fears about what was happening. I remember him crying once and saying, 'I'm so grateful to you, John', and I just dismissed him and the tenderness of that moment, patted his hand and said, 'It's fine, I love you. I want to do this.' I wish I had just let him get that out, let that be a moment between us.

I knew I had to be strong for Robert and believe we were going to beat this. We were going to say that we'd fought and we'd won. The alternative was too hard to comprehend. But, at the end of 2008, a year punctuated by paramedics and pain relief, we knew something was up, and in March 2009 we were told Robert had three months to live.

I was in denial, still believing I could make a difference. I felt I could find alternative therapies and that I had some kind of divine ability to change our destiny. But everyone around us had an air of resignation, a look of 'The End' about them. Looking back now, I recognise that hanging on to life and our hopes and dreams came at a price. In our desperate fight to make it work, the rational part of our brains got switched off. I had completely disregarded my exhaustion.

Robert began to make peace with the fact that we would soon part company and that our dreams would not come true this time round. I was torn: driven not to give up on him, but keen to ensure that he was comfortable and could die with dignity. I desperately wanted to find that miracle, but deep down I began to realise that I had to let him go.

The day before Robert died a healer came to the hospice and she took me through a process called 'cutting cords'. She asked me to mime the act of cutting a cord in front of me with a pair of scissors. This would represent the tie between Robert and me. I broke down. Instinctively I knew that this symbolic act was my letting go, admitting defeat and facing the truth that Robert was going to die. I cut it, very reluctantly and felt wracked with guilt.

The next day, the decision was made to insert a syringe driver, the final stage of pain control which I knew would make him less conscious. I found this very difficult as I recognised that my last moments with the person I adored were being taken away from me. I felt so powerless. Robert's family gathered around his bed and we kept him company while he slowly became unconscious. We played songs he loved on the CD player and reminisced on the fond memories that we had with him. Soon after Michael Buble's 'Home' finished playing, Robert expelled his last breath and I remember turning to his sister and saying, 'I think he's just died.'

What Does It Feel Like?

I felt a split second of panic. The phrase buzzed around in my mind, 'He's just died'. I suddenly had a desperate desire to have taken Robert's place. I remember thinking how strange it was that everyone had sat so calmly with this semi-corpse, just moments before, but when that final breath had gone, everything seemed to change. It's like a great collective wail, a combined grief. I stayed there for a bit and just sat with my sense of failure. I began questioning all the things I'd put my hopes on, thinking I could have made a difference. An overwhelming sense of emptiness overcame me. I felt numb. When I walked out of the room, Robert's brother came and gave me a hug and I cried. But I wasn't me. I was on autopilot. I was shell-shocked.

I left soon after and went home for a shower. I had the weirdest feeling as I walked through the house into the hallway. Even though I'd been there before without Robert, this time it was suddenly completely empty of his presence. And yet it was also filled with memories, snippets of conversations scattered around. I found myself in that post-holiday mode, thinking: ten minutes ago I was next to him; a week ago he was lying on the sofa with me watching a movie.

When I got back to Robert, it was a relief to be able to sit with his body. Suddenly it was silent. The noise of the moments after death had disappeared. His presence was gone, but the room somehow felt full of our time together and love for each other.

It didn't take long after Robert had died for me to feel the futility of what we had just gone through and the pain of my loss. I started thinking about the cumulative pain Robert had experienced over the last four years. I found myself asking,

'Why?' and felt I was entering into a serious existential crisis. When Robert was unwell, I'd tried everything I could to make him better: I took a course in reiki healing in the hope it would cure him; I learned Wicca, Bach flower remedies, reflexology – I wanted to be the one who would make that difference. It felt like my mission. When Robert died, I began questioning whether it had been worth putting so much effort into things that were unproven? I was angry, frustrated and disillusioned. I couldn't believe I'd invested so much of my energy in these practices and none of them had delivered.

This anger brought out a very practical part in me, and that part wanted to kick the whole issue out of my system in order to cope – so I occasionally appreciated it when people ignored what had happened. But there was also another part of me that really wanted to connect with Robert's essence and my emotional experience of loss.

I knew that this meant I was a walking contradiction and it was, therefore, very hard for people to help me. My normal demeanour vanished. I was more cutting, angry, critical on the one hand, and yet given to crying at the drop of a hat on the other. I was also less tolerant of situations that I was not comfortable in and in the company of individuals I didn't connect with.

What Can You Say – And Avoid Saying?

I was conscious that people around me didn't feel they could talk openly about death and loss, and that they seemed to stumble when I needed sincerity. I became resigned to the fact that people couldn't handle it but I have often wondered what pain could have been released if someone said to me 'Just be with your pain, John.'

I was grateful when people simply told me they were there for me, and that if I needed anything I just had to ask. It felt reassuring to know that I wouldn't be forgotten – that if I realised what I needed, I could turn to someone. And it was good to know that if I stumbled, or felt alone, I had people who would be there. But I wasn't fully aware of what I needed. I needed space and yet I felt lonely. Don't be put off if you recognise these kinds of conflicts in someone who is grieving. The best thing is to be open-minded and remember that what they want one day might not be right the next.

The most grating thing people tended to say was that they knew how I felt. It felt so insulting. They didn't know. They had no concept of the depth of pain I was feeling, and to dismiss it by saying they knew, felt like they were taking away the opportunity for me to talk about it and, frankly, it felt disrespectful.

'Time will heal' was another well-used phrase. This may indeed be true, but in the moment, it gives no consolation. It only somehow cements the reality of the situation – and especially at the beginning when you might be in denial. I also didn't want to believe that with time, the importance that Robert played in my life would diminish, that our time together was over.

With colleagues, it was different – my practical side kicked in and I could behave like nothing had happened. So from them, questions like 'How are you?' were actually encouraging; they appealed to the fix-it in me – the bit that wanted to come out of it all OK.

It was with Robert's family – my surrogate family – that I was hoping for a space where we could share a mutual loss, explore our grief more effectively. His parents seemed to be putting on the front of 'he isn't suffering anymore' and so it was never really allowed to just be shit. If you don't allow the bereaved person to express the shit-ness of the situation, it can be quite isolating for them.

I think because I also wore my "I'm OK" mask with my friends much of the time, they had to ask how I was doing before they got to see what was inside. With his family I hoped I could drop the mask and share my pain and anguish openly. The fact that I couldn't there either was difficult.

What Helped – and What Didn't?

I was not an easy griever – I needed to be heard when I wanted to air my pain, but my need for privacy kept people at arm's length. I wanted people to help me figure out how to feel all my conflicting emotions, while giving me my own space to lick my wounds: 'Stay by me, but keep out!' Not surprisingly, my friends didn't know quite how close they could get to me (or how close they wanted to be), but as awkward as I was, there was always support when I needed to connect. Most times, all they could do was sit with me and watch me weep; just sharing and being with the powerlessness of the situation. I needed to be reassured that that was OK for them, too. Phone-calls, dinner and coffee meets were gratefully offered, as long as they were on a flexible basis. I needed to know I could change my mind at the last minute.

What helped was trusting that my friends could be flexible in their support and have the courage to be vulnerable with me; to be brave enough to coax me out of my shell and know that if I responded negatively, it's not an attack on them. In most cases this is what I did experience.

Certain places were crammed with memories and I found myself making pilgrimages to these places to recapture the memories that we shared there. I would go and sit with Robert's body in the chapel of rest or sit in the hospice, or go to the crematorium. Once or twice I asked people to accompany me, but I would get them to wait for me outside. I was grateful that my friends would be there waiting for me, and that they didn't get offended by me asking them to wait somewhere else.

Women friends were more open to crying with me and they also hugged me more, but this wasn't always what I wanted. There were times when I felt that a hug was stifling or even unsafe while I was in that vulnerable state. At such moments a hug would probably have evoked feelings of anger or resentment. It's best to simply ask what the person needs in these moments. If their emotions seem all over the place don't make any assumptions.

Robert's brother and I were the main organisers of the funeral. He was very pragmatic and I was grateful for his support. Robert's mum contributed financially, his sister helped to choose the coffin and we all planned the ceremony together. I was in a haze throughout the organisation, so I didn't get that cathartic experience people often talk about with funerals. It was all kind of go, go, go; just ticking jobs off the list with no sense of it being a positive process in any way. I felt under enormous pressure to maintain control because I wanted to do Robert proud. I forced myself to be strong, which meant I didn't break down until after the ceremony when he'd gone to the crematorium. We had the wake at his mum's. I wanted to break away from it all; I needed my space. I didn't want to be a wailing banshee at the funeral and I didn't want friends to encourage me to cry.

There were some awkward moments of silence where people clearly didn't know what to do, but on the whole I felt supported. Friends made small talk, and commented on how well the wake was going. Others spoke of their memories of Robert, some laughed, some cried. Some hugged me while others told me, 'Now's the time to look after yourself.' As long as the act comes from the heart, with sincerity and compassion, it will be the best support that you are ever able to offer.

My family live abroad, so they couldn't be with me. I remember calling my mum, breaking down and asking, 'Will I get to see him again, Mum?' I don't remember her answer, but it didn't matter – it was just about having her hold that moment for me on the phone and not judge me for asking the question.

Because my family weren't there to help, I was that much more dependent on Robert's. And as much as they were very protective and caring towards me, a small part of me felt like an outsider looking in on their grief. There was a very subtle sense of exclusion, and I can't say for sure if it was my cutting off from them or if it's a natural phenomenon.

Acquaintances were the first to drift off. Then work colleagues. Friends followed, but more gradually. Society dictates a certain time for you to grieve but don't leave it up to the family to keep the space open for the bereaved person to talk about it. Make a point of checking in later down the line. They may choose to do their reconnecting privately, but the invitation would be appreciated I'm sure.

And Lastly ...

If truth be told, I wanted someone, anyone, to take the pain away, but no one can do that. So just let there be space to share memories of the dead person. Be patient. I know I must have been a pain in the arse; I was so all over the place. So love the person who has lost someone enough to give them space and to let them be whoever they need to be.

What you can learn from John's story

John's experience teaches us a lot about the confusing nature of grief. Indeed extrapolating practical tips from his story after interviewing him was a challenge for us both. But I don't think this aspect of grief need be a hindrance to supporting a friend like John. The key is compassion and adaptability. Don't let your friend's confusion destabilise you in your role – in fact, take it as sign that stability and consistency is probably more necessary. That doesn't mean consistent hugs and visits, but regular reminders you're still available – that whatever it is they need on that day is OK with you.

I also think John's story clearly demonstrates how important it is for supporters to work on feeling comfortable with their own vulnerability in order to 'hold' the vulnerability of others. John wasn't able to express his very often, but when he did, it was crucial that it wasn't met with discomfort and awkwardness. Accept your powerlessness in these circumstances – you can't fix your friend or make it better, but you can be there in that painful space with them. And that may well be all they need.

Finally, John talks of how he needed various types of support from his different networks. He wanted colleagues to mostly ignore it but with Robert's family he wanted it to be entirely about the death. So don't judge what your friend or loved one needs based on how they are in one particular setting. Be mindful that everyone will have their own unique role to play in the support dynamic.

Chapter 5

Rose, whose brother died

My only brother, Sam, died in September 2011, in a car accident in which no other driver was involved. He was twenty-seven, three and a half years older than me, and my best friend.

Sam and I had always been really close. We were in the same theatre company outside of school, which formed the basis of a shared social life. We also identified with each other because we both found certain areas of our relationships with our parents difficult. Our parents knew how close we were and depended on it because they knew we could diffuse almost any tense family situation – we just worked really well together.

We were an army family. Dad had been in the army and it was always clear that Sam was heading the same way. When he eventually decided to join up, we were really happy for him. It felt natural. Of course, it did make me think about what I'd do if he died. But whenever I worried about it, I forced myself to think about something else. It just wasn't an option.

Sam had been back from Afghanistan for a year. Mum had been holding her breath for the six months he was away and she'd finally let go. He was back and he was safe. Sam and I had spoken the night before he died and he'd told me he was going for a drive the next morning – he loved his car. He did just that and it killed him. We don't really know what happened. We know he overtook someone, and it's possible he clipped a drain near where he was found, but all we know for certain is that he veered off the road and hit a tree. Nothing else seemed to have hit the car. He was wearing his seatbelt and his phone was in the glove compartment. We were told it was impact injuries. I hope to God it was instant. That's my biggest fear; that he died slowly, and alone. I've been to the site of the accident once. I don't know if I'll go again.

If someone is in the army, the army is responsible for informing the family of their death, regardless of whether or not they were on army duties at the time. Mum told me that when the two men in black walked up the drive she thought there must be a mistake because, of course, Sam was not at war. This was one of the worst cruelties. He'd dodged bullets in Afghanistan and was really good at it, then he'd come home, we all thought he was safe, and his car hit a tree. That was the error – thinking he was safe.

As soon as my parents had been informed, the colonel, who had been timing the whole process, called my dad and asked what he needed. He said the only thing he needed was for them to find me, and that I shouldn't be alone when I found out. So the colonel deployed two men, Sam's boss and his best mate, to head to Cambridge where I was living. They rang the doorbell, ready with my Dad on the other end of the phone, only to find I wasn't there.

I was with a friend at a concert in London and half way through I nipped out to check my phone. I had one text from my dad saying, 'Where are you hiding, kid? Call me, love you.' I had another from my ex-boyfriend saying: 'Rose, I'm so sorry to hear about your brother, if there's anything I can do.' My heart stopped. I called my dad and shouted down the phone, begging him to tell me what had happened. He wouldn't say anything until I'd gone in to get my friend. Then I just screamed.

We got a taxi back to Cambridge to meet the army boys. As soon as we arrived I asked which one of them was George, my brother's mate, and threw myself into his arms. I guess I took comfort in the fact that he'd been close to my brother. What I didn't know then, but found out later, was that he had identified my brother's body; such an incredibly brave thing to do, and so generous.

My friend stayed with me all the way back to Yorkshire. The journey alternated with moments of hysteria and calm. If I started crying, George would reach his hand back to mine to comfort me. Unfortunately, it marked the beginning of a very unhealthy and strange relationship, which ended a few months later.

What Does It Feel Like?

The moment I got home, I waded in and said to my parents, 'Don't worry about this, guys. I'll sort it all out.' And they let me. I felt an instinctive need to be strong for them, but it's only now that I look back and wonder how I kept going. I took on a lot of responsibility. I took complete control of calling all of my brother's friends (and there are many) and breaking the news to them. It was a huge undertaking. My parents were caring, but I felt it definitely affected our future relationship quite badly, and it's not one I can now depend upon in the way that I used to. I know it's not their fault, but it's hard. I felt a need for something from them that wasn't met – an implicit understanding that I had lost someone, too. I think that's partly why I was drawn to George; I needed my own person who was there just for me.

I reacted in a way that was quite characteristic of me – somehow staying calm, with resolution and determination. Of course, it would have been impossible to cry constantly with a pain as big as this anyway, but I also tried not to fight the tears all the time, and I forced myself into counselling too. I couldn't find a way to communicate what I needed to my friends, and then I often felt guilty because I wasn't helping them to help me. I think I was also frightened about losing more people and didn't want to burden them. So counselling was great in that way because I felt totally 'allowed' to be myself.

Most people were shocked at the way I coped I think, and this meant they didn't know what to do. People expect a certain thing from grief and are therefore only prepared for that, so when someone is seemingly coping quite well (note the 'seemingly') they tend to flounder.

I was actually utterly lost. I didn't know who I was any more. It was such an acute emotion I didn't think I would survive. I'd lost my identity. I felt like half my body had gone. I didn't know how to operate. I felt like I couldn't see myself any more, like I was totally enveloped in this grief and that I – as I'd known myself – had ceased to exist. I was terrified about who to 'invest' in. What if they let me down? What if they left me too? It felt safer to do it on my own.

I wanted to go back to work quite soon after Sam died, as I didn't really have anything else to do. None of my friends lived nearby and the army were taking care of almost everything, so it left us with very little to do. Mum and Sam's girlfriend busied themselves with photos and memories, but I didn't take any comfort in being close to things that reminded me of him. I had enough in my head and that was torturous. I didn't feel close to him in Cambridge; maybe that's why it felt a bit easier being at home.

I have very few blood relatives, and only one aunt and uncle I really know well. Therefore, I've been very close to them in

50 SPEAKING OF DEATH

the past few years, as was my brother. My aunt has no children and my uncle has very problematic relationships with his, so my brother and I seemed to fill a hole in their lives, and they love us both very dearly. When Sam died it became very difficult to communicate with them, as they were both so terribly devastated by what had happened, but were in a different position from my immediate family. That relationship is still difficult.

What Can You Say – And Avoid Saying?

I was always quite capable of talking about Sam's death, to the point where I feared people couldn't handle it. They'd ask questions and I'd talk openly and then see the look of terror on their faces. This often made me feel like I should stop talking.

Sometimes I worried that if I chose to share my experience of loss with someone it would sound like I was trying to trump them in some way. It can often shut down the conversation because the recipient thinks I will then want to talk about it and they then feel they can't continue with their own story. Don't assume the bereaved person doesn't want to hear about you. It is possible to tell someone of your loss and then move on to talking about something else. It might be just what they need.

Equally, don't feel you can't tell the bereaved your own troubles and painful experiences just because you might not think they're as 'bad'. My boss, who has been phenomenal and has been there for me through everything, did exactly this. Her husband was made redundant shortly after I returned to work and she started crying to me when she got the call. For me, it was a real moment of crossing boundaries, in a positive way – I was there, giving her a cuddle, and she was crying. But then, suddenly, she looked up and said, 'But you know what, in the grand scheme of things, this isn't as bad ... ' I was so upset. I knew she meant well, but I really didn't need her to bring it back to how much worse my life was.

Also, a lot of people – particularly in the older generation – seemed to flounder. Or they would just be a little bit over-the-top with me, giving melodramatic displays of comfort and reassurance that just didn't feel very genuine. I also didn't need to hear how well I was doing all the time. It sounds so patronising – and really they had no idea.

Over a year after Sam died I went on holiday and had a fabulous time. It was really healing. Inevitably, I got back with a bit of a bump (that's often the case, especially now). I was talking to John, a dear friend, about this and told him I was feeling a bit low. He asked, 'With what?' So I said, 'Well, with all the grief and everything.' He then asked, 'Oh, does that still bother you?' I couldn't even reply. I just gave him a look. I know it's not malicious and that he's always struggled with this. He just can't get his head around the longevity of grief – the fact that it's still going on and that maybe I can't be there for him and his problems as much as I might have been before. This is a problem every single day, in some way.

Someone else – a girl who I hadn't seen for years, who had a brother the same age as Sam – said to me at the funeral: 'I only live round the corner from my brother, but I never see him ... makes you think really. Maybe I should see him more, just in case.' My internal response was a little X-rated, but all I could do was to thank her for attending.

A friend once asked me if grief felt like concussion. I know he was just trying to understand, but it felt so wrong for someone to try to make a direct comparison with something that was so insignificant. There is no way for me to describe it. It's an ever-changing thing. It feels different today, to tomorrow, to yesterday. It takes a very clear-headed individual to see it distinctly in the moment. I can see periods of time, and shifts here and there, but I can only see those changes now when I look back. Where it sits in my life now is too big to describe, so I would say it's probably best not to ask the bereaved to label their grief, unless they appear to be attempting to themselves.

Of course, my friends also brought enormous comfort with their words. John had a knack of bringing up all the terribly crass things people had said at inappropriate times, which made me laugh, but he did tend to stumble when laughing wasn't an option. Humour can be great, and our family made people feel enormously uncomfortable at times with all sorts of dark jokes, but it isn't always ideal.

One friend, who had never experienced anything like this, told me that to her it seemed a bit like being reborn – as though I was coming into an utterly different world, as a new person, and so of course it would take time to get used to it. This came from her genuine experience of me and was so accurate. It was such a great thing to say.

I quite like talking now to people I don't know because they don't probe. There was a time when I'd have avoided those conversations, wary of the inevitable sibling question. But now I'll try and pre-empt it, dropping it in as an aside – 'Well, we used to do that, but he died a few years ago' – so they know we don't need to talk about it, and that I'm OK with it. Sometimes that can be exhausting though.

What Helped – and What Didn't?

Sam was my one secure thing in life. That's what hurt. He was the one person I trusted more than anyone, and I had no idea how I was going to cope without that. Mum was reacting so differently from me: she made a calendar of photos of him and gave one to everyone ... I know that was her way, but I just didn't get it as a concept. His girlfriend made a collage too and put it up in her flat. I couldn't bear to look at it. Even now I can only have photos with sort of half his face. It's just too intense. Why would I put my face in the fire when I'm sitting that close? That's why I get frustrated. I still find it difficult that there are photos of him everywhere at home; I walk in the door and I'm confronted by a shrine. And all I see is why it's there. I dread it every time I go home. But it's their house now. It's where they grieved. And that's another casualty of Sam's death – because I lost my home too. Or what it used to mean to me. I have had to re-categorise it, like a lot of things.

The most important moments were when my friends remained consistent when they were with me. It reminded me that I was still in there somewhere, even if I felt like I was going mad. Don't be too influenced by the mood of the bereaved person. It will change, but your consistency will keep them steady.

I had a falling out with my best friend because I needed her more than the others and she seemed particularly absent. It felt to me that she wasn't being attentive, but she explained that she just hadn't known what to do – she was busy, and was trying to treat me normally; she'd thought that I would text her if I needed her. I explained that I couldn't do that – that I didn't know how to ask for help. I think we needed that argument. It gave us an insight into each other and we now have an amazing relationship.

Another friendship really suffered though, and with that one I just had to say enough is enough. First, she couldn't come to the funeral because she needed to look after her kids. Then, for Sam's birthday my mum organised a big party, and this friend told me that she couldn't come because she'd cut her hand. When we spoke about it later she explained that she was in the most horrendous, constant underlying pain. 'You must know how it feels, Rose', she said. I was flabbergasted. I couldn't believe she was comparing my grief to a pain in her hand. You can forgive friends, but after a while you start thinking, how many times should I have to?

A couple of months after Sam died John came to visit me. We had dinner, drank quite a bit and I talked. Then, inevitably, the tears began. And instead of stopping, I kept talking, and looked up to find John crying with me – not trying to stop me, or stop himself, or hug me, but just crying with me. It was the perfect thing to do at that moment.

On the whole, I preferred not to be hugged by someone when I was crying. Then I could sit back with their reassurance, 'It's OK, keep crying'. Often it's not a cry that can be fixed with a hug – it's the sort of half-hour crying stint that just needs to come out.

The funeral experience was very unusual as the army took care of all the procedures. On the one hand, it was incredible to be so looked after and to know that there was always someone we could call if we needed anything, but it also made it very hard to fill the time in the two weeks between his death and the funeral. We found ourselves with very little to do except stare this hideous grief in the face. Seeing that everything on the practical side was in hand, people focused instead on keeping us as busy as possible in other ways. We started a massive jigsaw on our dining-room table – a huge, beautiful picture of snow leopards. I'm not sure if we ever finished it but it was the perfect thing. Everyone got involved and it was really good to have something else to stare at. It was about all our brains could handle.

Sam was cremated, and now he's in the wood that my parents own in Yorkshire. I didn't want him to be there, but my parents made the decision without asking me. What's more, when we were standing by the spot where we'd buried Sam's ashes, Dad said, 'There's the space for us then'. I was aghast, thinking, It's going to be me putting you in there! I then felt even more isolated and alone.

I did make new friends through this experience and I'm still doing so. I recently met someone at a party whose younger brother committed suicide two months after Sam died; I'd heard that this girl was grieving in a very different way to me – not talking about it, partying a lot – and that her friends were worried. But one day she just suddenly opened up to me about it, which did both of us a lot of good; it was one of those 'Oh-you-do-that-too/oh-good-I'm-not-going-mad' moments. Since then, we've been out for dinner together, and sat eating, drinking and crying. It's comforting for each of us just to know the other is out there, but it's too much for me to do all the time. I can't pretend with her, and sometimes I just need to be able to put on a brave face and not be pulled up on it. Most of my friends do allow that because they recognise that it's something I need to do in order to cope. It's important for me that they understand this is a perfectly normal reaction, and a way of surviving, especially at the beginning.

I've also become closer to some people, who perhaps I didn't know as well before my brother died. Forming new friendships and relationships when one is so vulnerable can make each new bond feel very potent, but it is sometimes hard to judge the authenticity. At a time when I didn't even trust myself or know how I was changing, I found it hard to trust new people. I worried that they'd form their judgement of me around my story – that the friendships would be based upon my grief and their desire to help. I feel like I need to wait for the point when it becomes a more manageable part of me, and not everything I am. So I guess new friends need to be incredibly patient and not smother the grieving person with sympathy the whole time.

Now I look back and think, 'God, I was so high maintenance sometimes'. I needed a lot more than I would ordinarily, but didn't always know what that was. I wanted to be treated normally, but not to the extent that friends didn't ring more than usual. I wanted them to check in with my grief, but not *only* about my grief. At one point, I began to feel my friends would ring and only want to talk about Sam, being too nervous to talk about themselves. I found this so frustrating; I wanted people to ring with their own problems too. I guess the fundamental quality I needed then, was for friends to be flexible and accommodating, and once again, patient. And all my friends really were this way most of the time. But the tricky thing is that sometimes nothing hits the spot, and you can really only see that years down the line.

And Lastly . . .

When you speak to the bereaved person, let them know that it's fine for them to talk about it as much as they want. Know that they don't expect you to understand or get how it feels, but that it is enough to simply listen when they need you. Be consistent and reassure them that they can depend on you – so if you say you are going to call, make sure you do. Sometimes that one call can mean everything. If you forget, then for someone whose whole world has just imploded this can be more distressing than it would normally be.

What you can learn from Rose's story

This is a story about asking for help, and the spell that the appearance of strength can cast over the non-bereaved. The loss of a sibling at a young age will often force the remaining child into the role of chief supporter to their parents. This means their need for their own tailored care is likely to be greater.

Don't be fooled by their strength. Rose clearly kicked into coping mode with her parents and no doubt exuded strength and stability most of the time. That doesn't mean that she wasn't crumbling beneath the façade. Don't rely on the bereaved to tell you when they need help. Just give it, until they tell you not to.

Chapter 6

Julia, whose mother died

Mum died when I was thirty-five – suddenly and unexpectedly on 21 December 2010. At least, that's when we discovered her body.

It had been a typical run-up to Christmas until that point – parties, last-minute shopping and all the usual chaos. My last contact with Mum was at around 10 p.m. on Sunday the nineteenth, when we'd exchanged texts.

My brother was due to travel to Germany and needed to pick up a suitcase that was stored at Mum's place. Not having heard back from her on the Monday, he rang me on Tuesday to check if I'd heard anything before he headed over there. Mum worked as a carer and was incredibly independent. She was usually out until at least 9 p.m. most days, so I wasn't concerned.

That evening, my fiancé (now husband), Steve, and I were eating dinner while working our way through a TV box set. The phone rang. My brother's trembling voice said, 'You need to get here now.' When I asked what had happened he just said, 'The worst possible thing – please come now.'

Fortunately, we lived very nearby. When we were about two minutes away I called my brother to let him know we'd be there any moment. He told me the ambulance was going to wait until we got there. I thought this was weird – surely they should have sped straight to hospital? It was then that I was sure Mum had died.

'I think Mum's dead,' I said to my fiancé in a strangely matter-of-fact voice. When he burst into tears, saying, 'No, no, no', I felt surprised that my reaction wasn't the same – it was my mother, after all. But in that moment, it just felt like another piece of information.

I rushed into the house and found my brother with one of the paramedics. He must've told me that Mum was dead, at which point I ran upstairs to see for myself. My brother urged me to stop, saying it wasn't something he wanted me to see, but I couldn't accept the news until I knew with certainty that it was true. I needed to see how dead she was.

I found Mum collapsed on the floor, her face a duller shade than when I'd last seen it. (For months afterwards, when I thought of Mum I remembered her there on the floor.) I hugged her, crying and stroking her hair, then went back downstairs shortly after. I was suddenly acutely aware of the trauma my brother had just experienced and wanted to comfort him. I still can't imagine how horrendous it was for him to go bounding up the stairs, shouting, 'Mum!' only to find her like that.

The rest of the evening is a bit of a blur. My brother's girlfriend arrived at some point, and I remember hugging Steve closely as two men lifted Mum down the narrow staircase, trying to negotiate the tight turns without bumping into all the cat paraphernalia that lined it. The noises were almost comical, but we couldn't stop crying.

The paramedics said Mum had had a cardiac arrest (confirmed eventually by the autopsy) and the only small comfort was that her death would have been pretty instantaneous.

Unless a medic had been standing by her side, nothing could have saved her.

What Does It Feel Like?

My initial reaction was so matter-of-fact, it was almost clinical. It was like I was dealing with a crisis scenario at work, and that quite worried me. I was relieved when I was able to cry as it reminded me I was still human. That said it was a great coping mechanism. Given the amount of administration that was to come, I was quite grateful that I'd kept my head.

I spent most of my time with Steve, my brother and his girl-friend. We'd had a shared experience and each of us seemed to understand what the other needed. We were a self-contained little group and I liked it that way. I didn't want anyone else around.

I knew I had to tell my friends, but I didn't know how to do it. I didn't really want to talk about it because I was aware that any questions would be about the details of the event, rather than about me, and I thought that would annoy me. I couldn't handle the inevitable tedium of repeating the same story.

I decided that putting a post on Facebook was the best option – I could drop the bomb and then run away. I wrote: 'What a shit week. First my snowman's head falls off and then my wonderful, eccentric mother dies.' I was amazed at the response to such a typically British way of disguising emotion. I was so impressed at how well brought up people were!

I felt mostly guilt for a long time after Mum died. Not just because I hadn't called her, but because my brother and I were now legally obliged to visit her house every week in order to keep the insurance valid, which made us realise how easy it would have been to visit her more often. There was something very wrong about going round to her house so regularly once she was dead.

I retreated into myself a lot and was aware that I wasn't very much fun to live with. It would have been easier if I'd reacted more like Steve – if I'd been more openly distressed – but I was quietly grieving and I didn't know how to do it any other way. At one point Steve said he was worried I was avoiding my grief. And I probably was avoiding the emotions, but that was my way of surviving. I wasn't in denial – I knew she was dead – I was just trying to hold back the tidal wave.

My natural reaction was to try to do everything on my own. I'm a bit of a control freak anyway, but also, the more I did myself, the less anyone else had to be involved and therefore the less I'd have to talk about it. It took me nearly two years before I could mention that Mum was dead 'casually' in a sentence without getting a massive lump in my throat and going into a bit of an internal panic.

So avoidance tactics seemed to work for me. When thoughts of Mum sprang into my head I would force myself to think of something else. It was incredibly powerful. I learned to look upwards to push back the tears; I would save them all up, then go to the loo, have a good cry and then pretend it hadn't happened. I'd also ask people loads of questions – it's amazing how they will go along with you, if you ask them about themselves. I just withdrew from the world, but there did come a point when I knew I couldn't keep it in for ever, otherwise I'd just get a massive headache.

What Can You Say – and Avoid Saying?

Being reminded repeatedly that Mum had died young wasn't helpful, and I often found I had to comfort the comforter. The reactions of people of my mum's generation were especially difficult for me because it was totally about them: 'Oh my God; I'm the same age as her.' They would be caught up in that moment of realising their own mortality, and, again, I'd end up reassuring them.

I also found it hard to gauge how authentic people were. I shouldn't think that any of my friends' motives were anything other than the best, but a part of me felt that the multiple questions that inevitably followed the news were a bit voyeuristic – like people rubbernecking on the motorway.

Three work colleagues I was not previously close to were particularly great. They had all lost a parent, so they were able to tell me their experiences and their timescales. I wanted 'facts', so I took great consolation in hearing simple things – that I wouldn't forget my memories, that the pain when I thought of her would gradually lessen over time and that as the shock sunk in I'd cry less regularly.

It seems ridiculous that when you lose someone you can still worry that you're grieving 'incorrectly', but I did. There seemed to be so many ways and rules, and I wasn't really clear about mine, so I got quite self-conscious. I found Elisabeth Kübler-Ross's five stages of grief comforting. I liked that they formed an accepted, professional view; and it meant I could reassure myself that because I hadn't 'done' all of the stages, my grief didn't have to be finished.

Lots of old school friends wrote lovely random messages on Facebook, which made me smile. It was good to know that even people who hadn't seen Mum for over twenty years still got in touch and shared fond memories of her.

I was moved by how many cards we got from friends and neighbours, especially those that had clearly been chosen to reflect Mum's tastes (ones with cats on them, for example). There can be a tendency to use overly formal language when writing to someone about a loss, and while every card we received was hugely appreciated, more personal words like, 'Your mother was a wonderful woman and you clearly inherited your positivity and strength at least in part from her' perhaps made a bigger impact and brought more comfort than words like, 'Our deepest sympathy on the loss of your mum'.

It was strange going back to work. I valued the sense of purpose, but it was pretty awkward. The six people in my team all knew what had happened, but we were part of a bigger set-up with people who didn't know. So in the post-Christmas office banter of those first few weeks back at work I withdrew a lot. I thought if I came across as quiet, then people would leave me alone. I didn't care if they thought I was weird.

I found it much easier to talk to people about it on the phone. My managing director asked me lots of questions and there was something about the way she asked them – her tone, the gentleness of her voice – that told me they weren't coming from a place of nosiness. Also, on the phone you can avoid the awkward faces, and it doesn't matter if you look like you're going to cry. It's a nice, protective cloak. I'd find myself having twenty-minute conversations with a client I usually struggled to chat with about my fear of forgetting Mum. Yet I couldn't – and wouldn't – talk about it with some of my closest friends. I think I figured I spent enough time with my head filled with Mum-related thoughts and that I needed my friends to distract me.

What Helped – and What Didn't?

I had no idea what I needed from people around me. I started to panic irrationally about whether I had to write down every memory I had of her just in case I forgot. I made a point of saving every text I still had on my phone and even her voicemail message to desperately try to keep hold of every link with her. My brother helped with this by connecting me to a programme that allowed me to store all her messages on my computer. I was grateful that these strange rather pointless attempts to manage my emotions weren't ignored or laughed at.

The process of preparing the funeral was fun. We had something to do and we had a purpose. Mum had written in her will: 'Think of something funky for my service, you two! No priests, no flowers – just a small cat figure from my children [we ended up getting a wreath that resembled a cat we'd had in our childhood] – no people, except my family in Spain, just my two children with their chosen "moral support" friends.'

My 'moral support' friends were two of my best school friends who had lost their parents to cancer in the previous year. I remember that when we talked about the upcoming funeral they both said they would be there to take care of any organising in the background. They didn't ask if they could – they simply stated that they were going to be there. I found that deeply reassuring.

Following Mum's instructions made the funeral organisation rather like an art project. She wanted an eco-coffin but, bizarrely, the Co-op didn't have any, so we had to use a hideous giant cardboard one. The coffin was in the house for over a week (probably the most cathartic thing we did was to decorate it) and we missed it when it was gone – it's hard not to see the funny side of life when you're eating dinner with a cardboard coffin in the corner of the room!

The only hitch in the whole process was when it came to deciding what would go in the coffin with Mum. My brother's girlfriend had made some lavender marmalade that she really wanted to go in there. I hated the idea that Mum's ashes would have glass and sticky stuff in with them, so I put my foot down and said no. It was obviously important to her, but I absolutely did not care. I wasn't sympathetic to her grief and this was the most selfish thing I did during that time. I put it at the back of Mum's cupboard and I've never been able to throw it away! I'll probably have it till I die now.

The funeral was a very personal event and anything else would have felt awkward, so it was great to know we could arrange it in a way that we were comfortable with. But it was after the funeral that we really needed the distractions to continue. One of my fiancé's relatives offered us the key to her place to come and go as we wished if we felt like a change of scenery. While we didn't take her up on it on this occasion, we did find it hugely valuable to leave home for a few days at other times, and distance ourselves slightly from the overwhelming tsunami of emotions.

Another friend, meanwhile, sourced tickets to *Cirque de Soleil* and invited us out just ten days or so after the funeral. I think this was very brave, as others might have assumed that we weren't ready for it. And we weren't sure if we were either. But it gave us an excuse to leave the house for a no-pressure evening at a time when we might not otherwise have done so, and it was exactly what we needed.

The upside of losing someone when you're a bit older is that your friends can help more practically. Mum had hand-written her will and had used several swear words in it (about our dad, whom she'd divorced acrimoniously years before). Being an official document it had to be obscenity free, and this made it a somewhat trickier process than it might otherwise have been. However, a lawyer friend of mine happens to specialise in probate matters, so she got one of the girls on her team who's more junior to do it for a very reasonable fee. It made life so much easier.

In the few weeks after someone dies, there's an immediate rush of cards and messages, then once the funeral is over the attention starts to wane. Perhaps that's when you need it more though. It's like a sort of graph of presence, with the number of people you're surrounded by slowly and gradually diminishing over time. You feel like you should have moved on – and you have – but it can feel like you should have moved on more; as though everyone else thinks you're dwelling on it. I'm not the most touchy-feely person, and so people generally didn't need to do anything different physically. In fact, I probably went out of my way to avoid hugs for fear that they'd make me cry.

I didn't want people to constantly talk about it, but I think you need a bit of stability and continuity to help you get through tragedy, and it was difficult when people started to drift. I was a little surprised that none of Mum's friends ever followed up with us afterwards, to see how we were or to drop us a note around her birthday. I'm sure they were thinking of her, but it might have been nice to know.

Some of the most helpful things people did didn't involve trying to talk about Mum – for example, gestures of inviting us to the theatre to get us out of the house and help show that life goes on.

It's important the bereaved are in the company of people they feel totally safe with, but this might not always be who you'd expect. Sadly, my dad was someone we had to avoid around the time of mum's death because we knew his presence would change the dynamics. The most important thing was for us to feel free to cry, laugh, talk about Mum or just sit in silence – whatever we needed.

I did feel a bit of a temporary rift with some of my closest friends who went unusually silent during the first year. I was angry with them for not having tried harder and for not getting in touch more, but eventually I decided it must be because they hadn't been through anything similar themselves. And they probably didn't even realise how I felt, as I didn't bring it up with them. I was the one who had an issue with their reaction and that was my problem, not theirs. We're all fine now.

As far as work was concerned – it took about three months before they told me that they'd noticed my performance had dropped a bit and that my attitude wasn't as positive as it should be (funny that). That definitely felt premature.

And Lastly . . .

The grieving process is so depressing and all-consuming. Try to offer any opportunities for joy that you can, whether it's laughing at shared memories or getting the bereaved person out of the house to be distracted by a show for a few hours. Social gatherings might seem awkward (everyone knows, but no one really knows what to say), but it's important that life isn't put entirely on hold. Then again, if they're someone who needs to lie in bed and cry, then this approach may not be appropriate. But I think it is still nice to create happy memories with friends and family during that time of mourning, so that you can reflect on them later.

I still don't know exactly what 'the right thing' to do is when friends go through a similar thing – all I know is that you need to stay in contact, even if only by text, email or even Facebook, if you're too nervous to call. It's far worse dealing with grief when you think you've been abandoned by the outside world as well as your loved one.

What you can learn from Julia's story

The first lesson you can take from this story is about the use of questions. Telling people the news of your loved one's death can be exhausting but is also often something of a release. But if every time you tell someone, you are bombarded with questions about the details of the death, rather than how you are coping, the whole experience shifts from being potentially healing, to something one dreads. I know I have talked about being confident with your curiosity, but be curious with tact, especially when the curiosity is actually coming from a place of panic, rather than caring interest. Don't use questions about the details of the death as a shield to offering your support. Ultimately, the important point is the loss, not the way in which the person died.

This story also tells us something about the types of relationship the bereaved person may need. Having lots of people isn't necessarily the goal, it's about the quality of the company and the safety that each of those relationships represent to the mourner.

Finally, just because your bereaved friend or loved one doesn't want to talk about it and doesn't appear to be grieving, doesn't mean they don't need you around more than normal. Support is not just about wiping tears away, and lending an ear, its often just about hanging out together and putting extra effort into making your friend feel nice.

Chapter 7

Adam, whose best friends died

Peter and Eve were killed in a terrorist attack on the flight to their honeymoon destination. I had been the best man at their wedding. They were my closest friends and I loved them like a brother and sister.

I first met Peter when I was in my thirties. We were both musicians in different bands but it wasn't until a few years later, when we started working together, that we clicked as best friends. We had the same views on the world, the same taste in music and we wrote together, so we became incredibly close very quickly. Then he met Eve and we formed a great little unit.

Peter had asked me to look after his business while they were away on their honeymoon, and on the day they were due to travel, I couldn't get into his van, so I called him up for instructions. He was in a panic because they couldn't find Eve's passport. I remember him saying to me: 'If we don't find it in the next five minutes, we're going to miss the flight.' I can't count the number of times I have wished I'd kept him talking for a bit longer.

I went for a pint with a couple of friends after work that day, and for some reason we were all talking about Peter. I guess it was still not long after their wedding and we were all really excited for them, but I remember feeling intensely uncomfortable. Something felt terribly wrong. When I got home, I switched on the television and there it was – the news of the crash. I knew straight away. I felt numb.

I was with my wife and young daughter and we spent the rest of the evening on the phone, but because we weren't family members it was impossible to get any information. There was just the constant activity of making and receiving calls. I eventually got a call the following morning from Peter's housemate, confirming what I already knew, and I crumbled. I had that inevitable explosion, right from the gut. I had known all along, but I guess one still hopes against hope. It was pretty intense from that moment on. It was very dark.

What Does It Feel Like?

It was devastating for all of us left behind and because of the nature of their deaths, the trauma was protracted and very public. During the first two weeks I cried a lot. I felt heartbroken. Close friends are like family to me, and when you're in a band with someone it's like a love affair, so the loss felt the same. I didn't play any music for a long time. But it's hard as a friend, because you're cut adrift from the process. One day I hope it will encompass everybody – the whole community – but I felt I had to do my own intense grieving in private.

I hit the bottle quite a bit and cut myself off from the world. I didn't want anything from anyone. But after this initial 'poor-me' stint, which lasted maybe a couple of weeks, I found myself wanting to function again. I'd already experienced grief several times in my life, so I was very aware that if I wasn't careful, it could become really self-indulgent. My daughter was little, so I knew I had to keep the show on the road.

That's when I started to think I could give some support to Peter's parents. There was a lot of nuts-and-bolts stuff going on – practicalities and legal issues (because it was so public) – and I felt compelled to help. My wife and I went up to see them with my daughter. We'd only met them briefly before, but they were just the nicest people ever.

It was an honour to have been welcomed into Peter's family. We all became very close and I just did what I could for them. I talked to the press on their behalf (I had been in PR, so had some experience in this) and attended various meetings, like the support groups for the families affected.

Of course, they ended up depending on me a lot. I think to a certain extent this was because they knew I had been close to Peter, and so it gave them a sense of continuity. For my part, while helping so much on a practical level and supporting them by attending international support groups and investigative interviews on their behalf helped to make me feel engaged with the 'process', it also gave me no time for my own grieving. It became my way of coping. But, supporting them supported me. And I obviously talked about it more with them – that's what we connected on. We looked after each other. It was quite primal. And, with the family, I didn't have to worry about the notoriety of the circumstances. With my friends I was quite wary of people just wanting to 'get the goss', but with Peter's family I felt I had a safe outlet where the emphasis was simply on our loss.

What Can You Say – and Avoid Saying?

As soon as I found out, I got in touch with everyone I knew so that I didn't have to cope with them phoning me up and saying,

'Oh God, I've seen it in news ... they were your mates, weren't they?'

I found it insufferable that the press and even close friends were so frequently defining Peter and Eve by something that wasn't them – like their race or past achievements. It felt as though they were being diminished as people somehow. But on the whole, friends were so shocked by the event that generally they said very little, and frankly, I was quite happy for most people to just ignore it. Of course, the usual gallows humour jokes began to circulate, but I couldn't, in all conscience, be too offended. I know only too well that it's just a defence against horror, and I'm sure I would have been as bad as anybody else in different circumstances. Musicians tend to have a pretty grim sense of humour anyway.

On the whole, I didn't feel fragile. I felt confident in how I wanted to deal with it. I hated it when people did the, 'Oh-are-you-all-right?' thing, as soon as I walked in the room. I just wanted to be treated normally – to be able to get on with what we were doing. If I wanted to talk about it I would seek out the people I felt comfortable with, so I didn't need to be coaxed into it. I set the parameters of how I wanted things to be – perhaps it's a reflection of having experienced trauma before. So if someone started to talk about it with me in a particularly morbid way, I would say something like, 'And moving along now ...' I just couldn't be doing with weeping and wailing from anyone else. I guess my friends didn't all know that though.

Because of the public nature of the event, I was wary of people who weren't close to me. They had no connection and therefore any conversation with them felt wrong and almost a betrayal of Peter and Eve. A passing acknowledgement from casual acquaintances felt meaningless, and so it only irritated me. It needed to be grounded in something – in a conscious connection.

As for close friends and family, we were all connected in the same loss and grief. We didn't want to be hugged and moped over. I think we were all hurting too much. I know I certainly didn't want any drama. All people needed to say was, 'I've no idea what can be done, but I really am here. I am available to you for whatever it is you need.'

I'd have done anything to change the way they died. So I was often sensitive to that being talked about. I was also acutely aware of what it must be like to lose a child. It killed Peter's dad a few years later, I'm sure of it, so I was quite defensive with people who didn't seem to acknowledge the impact on Peter's family. I wanted them to be conscious of how bad it was for them, not me.

What Helped – and What Didn't?

It just happened that I was with Peter's parents when the first press call came through. It was obviously very upsetting for them, so that sort of established my role for them and I was happy to do it for them. I would have done anything I could for them. (It was difficult dealing with the other families though, especially those who wanted '*something* done', including attacking as yet unspecified countries which may or may not have been involved.) So it was important for me that people respected my choice to handle the trauma in this way, by helping Peter's parents, although I didn't care much if friends thought I should be dealing with it in other ways.

We had been planning to have some friends round for Christmas, but with Peter and Eve being killed just before then, I called to say that we weren't sure if we had the stomach to go through with the arrangement, and left it that we would see how we felt on the day. In the event, they arrived on our doorstep wearing silly hats and thrusting party poppers in our faces. I was taken aback at first, but then we all had a big cuddle and got on with the day. They judged it perfectly – we had as normal a Christmas as possible for the kids and were able to put real life on hold for a bit. I think the essence of what they did was to stay consistent. It was a reflection of how well they knew us and a real endorsement of our friendship. They knew we wouldn't want to be weeping and wailing. So I reckon the best thing you can do as a friend is to continue to be the way you've always been. We have every bloody Christmas with them now!

The wait for the funeral was unbearable. There was a separate service for Eve early on, organised by her parents, which I didn't go to. I just couldn't face it. I couldn't face God. I was cross and couldn't see how God came into it. Their double funeral was just wonderful though, although my memory of the day is clouded – I can't see anyone clearly somehow. I sat at the front, feeling a bit apprehensive and aware I was 'part of the family'. The coffins looked so tiny. I remember thinking about what could be inside them after that kind of death. It was grim.

What followed was the most extraordinary experience of my life, I think. The rabbi said a few words about both Peter and Eve, and then began to sing this kind of memorial prayer, this lament. It was the most mournful and moving thing I have ever heard, and was completely cathartic. It prompted uncontrollable weeping from the whole congregation; everyone broke down in tears – real gut-wrenching, agonising tears. It was the most amazing release and it somehow unlocked all the grief and loss and pain, which had been on hold since Peter's and Eve's deaths.

Afterwards, we were all left a little stunned, I think, and just moved from one small group to another, holding each other. I – and a lot of the congregation – was not used to public displays of emotion, so it came out of the blue and affected us on a really profound, visceral level. I didn't realise how much you need the catharsis of the funeral. But it felt so important. The sharing in it too. It's strange how crying is so powerful. I was reminded of a Joni Mitchell song that talks of crying and laughing as the same release. I would recommend that kind of lamenting to anyone.

Apart from that day at the funeral, I didn't get any hugs from my family, who were the only ones I really would have wanted that from. But I have a thing about hugs. How long should they last? There are people in your life you hug anyway, and they're OK, but I don't want unsolicited hugs from people. Cuddles are different. That's what I wanted from my dad – I wanted to be a baby and I don't see anything wrong with that. I didn't get it though.

I was aware of a more weary acceptance of what had happened among older people. The twentieth century gave us all plenty of experience in loss and grief, either first or second hand, so there seemed to be more of a collective understanding of the impact. This felt consoling in some way.

What I needed from people depended on my relationship with them. From my family I just wanted affection – to be cuddled and comforted. I was able to be vulnerable with my wife, but I was also aware that it can become corrosive, especially as she had lost them too, so you can end up indulging each other. So with my friends I wanted normality.

I think because of this, I didn't need to ask for help much. On the whole, I just wanted things to be the same and I guess for me to be allowed to grieve in my own way. And defaulting into being a helper was my survival thing – doing what I could in a hopeless situation.

Because I had put up this 'shield' against casual condolences I didn't really notice much drifting from supporters. I didn't allow myself to. There is a natural process, whereby people come together in a more intense way, but this can't, and should-n't, be sustained, and relationships should slowly fall back into normality. Any friendship born of trauma starts in an artificial way – you're starting in grief and support and I'm not sure how it can move on from there.

It felt that the most important thing was just to have people around and know they were there. Grief is essentially a soli-tary state and, like any healing, takes time and care. Nobody can 'heal' for you, just as nobody can feel pain in the same way as you, but I think it's important to be available, to let people know that you care unconditionally about their well-being, to be an emotional prop and to be a practical help if required.

I will always be furious at the insanity in the world that makes things like this happen, but concentrating on the why and how is pointless, and so I didn't want other people doing that. Nothing is going to bring Peter and Eve back.

And Lastly . . .

Misery loves company and there are people who are attracted to it. If you're a new friend of the bereaved, don't, however unwit-tingly, take advantage of their circumstances. Be respectful and aware that the friendship you build with them in that space is not necessarily sustainable, so don't be clumsy with their emo-tions.

What you can learn from Adam's story

This story gives us an insight into what it might feel like when a friend dies and the bereaved person is not one of the immediate family or 'inner circle' of mourners. While Adam obviously knew his friends intimately, his network of mutual mourners was relatively small. His role as consoler to the inner circle – the family – was clearly his way of supporting himself, but in turn it might have pushed his own friends away. Don't be put off by the inaccessibility of the inner circle of mourners. Let your friend find their own way, but stay close by for when they're ready to come back to you.

We can also learn a little about loss when it occurs in the public domain. It is possible that when someone has lost a loved one very publicly, they may be more likely to want the death ignored in their own private circles. Adam said a number of times he was wary of 'casual condolences'. I imagine because the bereaved will be surrounded by talk of the death much more than they might in more ordinary circumstances that distraction and normality may be the best thing you can offer for your friend.

Also, if you're not close to the bereaved person, accept it and don't try and forge a deeper friendship out of the mourning process.

Chapter 8

Nicola, whose brother died

My brother, Duncan, died in 1978, when he was seventeen, of the muscle-wasting condition, Duchenne muscular dystrophy, a disease which particularly affects males, but is only carried by females. He was diagnosed when he was three years old and I was nine.

My mum was very stoic and noble. She did everything she could for him, and Duncan was kept like a young child for all his seventeen years. He couldn't move himself, so had to be turned over in bed, meaning the nights were often disrupted. As a child he had difficulty walking, so he couldn't join in any games at school or at home, and by the time he was eleven years old, he was in a wheelchair. We never talked about it though. We just got on with life. Mum did things the way she thought best.

Everything in life had to be ordinary, so life was very predictable. We always knew when everything was going to happen and we never went anywhere unusual. It was very boring. That's my main childhood memory – of being very bored.

Muscular dystrophy doesn't affect the brain, which was more painful for us in some ways as Duncan was totally conscious and aware of what was happening to him. We got to know him incredibly well; he was a funny boy with a lovely nature, and he loved the television – that was his opening to the world. I guess in some ways it was easier for him that he was kept like a child – he hardly experienced adolescence, so perhaps he didn't feel so left out.

I had a pretty good relationship with Duncan, but sadly, Mum wouldn't let me or my sister, Lucy, look after him. She's a very strong Catholic, so I think she felt it was her burden; she felt guilty about it. Only when I met my husband, Matthew, a medical student at the time, did she let us look after him – in the last three years of his life. Our relationship improved then and I think it was nice for him to be with other young people instead of his parents. Of course, he used to get frustrated, but, on the whole, he was very resigned to his fate: he knew he was going to die – his older cousin had died from the same disease.

I was staying with a friend when Duncan died. I got a call from Matthew and I remember feeling so disoriented when I heard the news. I'd been shopping with my friend and couldn't stop thinking about the fact that I'd been trying on clothes while my brother was dying. There was also a weird feeling of numbness, a resignation that it had finally happened, that it was all over. This was followed by an overwhelming concern for my parents and a fear of whether I would be able to support them. I knew I had to be stronger than them, that it somehow just goes with the territory. But I wasn't sure if I could do it.

What Does It Feel Like?

Of course, we all knew Duncan was going to die; but we'd thought it would happen in his twenties because that was what we'd been told to expect, so it came as a shock. (Now sufferers can live till their forties.) He had started getting ill very frequently and he was going to hospital regularly to have his lungs drained, which he absolutely hated, so I think he decided he wasn't going to go on with it any more.

It was a very hard winter after he died. We were snowed in, and I remember thinking at the time, Thank goodness he died before. It would have been horrible for him. They were strange days between the death and the funeral. We had a dinner party every night; my father opened the best wine! I knew then and am still sure now it was his way of celebrating my brother's life. He didn't get to hospital in time before Duncan died, so it must have been very difficult for him. Mum was there with Duncan, so he left life as he came in – Dad wasn't at the birth either. Opening the best wine was his offering. He couldn't express the way he felt.

I liked the bubble that was created at that time because of how close we all were – it felt safe and strangely happy. As if Duncan was still with us in our midst. It was like being extra alive. I wonder if this is nature's way of keeping us going – making us almost more appreciative of 'being alive' – before the enormity of loss kicks in.

I didn't get to see Duncan after he died. I just went straight home, and then there was a lot of crying and wailing, mainly initiated by me. I have always been a bit of a crier. I remember seeing that the Hoover was in the middle of the sitting room and when I asked why it was there, Mum said, 'Papa was going to use it, but he didn't have the heart to in the end'. I found this spooky because I'd had a dream about Duncan dying, while Mum was vacuuming the sitting room, and in the dream I thought, 'Why is she doing that? My brother's just died.' That somehow added to the high emotions of the moment.

In the past, when I had imagined Duncan dying, I hoped that everyone would be calm and cope, and not rely on me for support. I was surprised at some of my reactions: I felt relieved, and then guilty at feeling relief. As a mother now, I find myself feeling keenly for my mum, who probably reserved her tears for her pillow at night.

In the days after his death, our immediate family was in a bubble of shock. Between the day of his death and the funeral we clung together, as though on a raft in turbulent seas after a shipwreck. It was in the days before mobile phones and the internet, so communication was less immediate. It was easy to disappear.

I felt quite alone. And I was alone. I was very locked in my own experience, so I didn't really notice how other people around me were behaving. I'd always been quite introverted, and I've never really shared much with my parents because they weren't really there: Mum was always busy with Duncan and Dad was often at work, so I think support for me from them just wasn't an option.

As a result, I wrote a lot in the days and weeks after he died. I had to delve into myself for support, seeking comfort from things like the weather (the sun was shining all of that first week). I remember going for early-morning walks and coming across a statue of a boy with a wolf – he looked just like my brother, but although made of stone his body appeared lean and agile. This made me cry.

I remember how few people addressed the subject of Duncan. They just avoided it. On the whole, I wasn't expecting help from other people because I knew it wasn't there.

My worry for my mum was dominant at that time. She'd given her whole life to looking after Duncan, so his absence must have been unbearable. I never saw her cry; she never cried in front of anyone. I didn't want to see her cry though, and I think she knew that. There was this unspoken arrangement between us, based on our experience of dealing with Duncan's illness: we'd never spoken about it – my parents had just silently coped – so because we had never talked openly and shared our pain before, we couldn't do it. It's only now, on reflection, that I can see this habitual dynamic we were locked into. We all kept to our roles, and mine was to be the highly strung odd one out, having screaming fits.

Matthew and I went to Paris for Christmas and I was so lonely when we got back. That was when it hit me. It was the finality that struck me the most – the realisation that Duncan's presence was forever lost and any attempt to keep it alive was futile. The world felt so cruel, going on as if nothing had changed – the sun still rising and setting, people going to and from work ... I remember a man followed me once and tried to pick me up, and I was completely outraged at his lack of sensitivity – as if he was to know!

What Can You Say – and Avoid Saying?

Although there was crying in the house, there wasn't much talk about the source of the pain. None of us talked about our feelings or shared our questions, our thoughts. Instead, we talked about my brother in the context of funny, sweet, moving anecdotes. In some ways I was grateful not to talk about the pain because I was afraid of seeing the vulnerable side of my parents. We were quite repressed as a family and I was always told off by my parents for showing emotion, so the prospect of seeing theirs felt scary. Someone told us that 'life must go on', but this was not how I imagined it would continue.

There were tons of letters in the days and weeks that followed, but astonishingly, not one of them was for me or spoke of what it might be like for my sister and me. I was struck by my hyper-sensitivity to this. Most letters paid lip service (e.g. 'to you and your family'), but very few people seemed to have considered the loss of a sibling. It seemed extraordinary. Mum would give us the letters to read and we'd scan them looking for our names which, if they were there at all, would only ever be at the end, as a token mention. Similarly, there were endless phone calls for my parents – so with no letters, no calls and surrounded only by family, I felt incredibly cut off from the world, and from my friends.

The letters ranged from very emotional, especially those from the French side of our family, to quite formulaic, from people who had never met my brother. Certain phrases and clichés cropped up frequently: 'It must be some consolation that he is now in a better place'; 'Our condolences on your loss'. People fall back on these stock phrases when they don't know what else to say, but I know it doesn't mean they don't care.

The more touching letters were those that really identified with what my mother might be going through, being specific about what it was like: 'the horrible waking in the morning, trying to sleep'. Knowing that my mum might find some consolation in these letters did, in turn, bring me some comfort. It somehow lessened the burden. But there is a difference between sharing in the pain and making someone else's pain your own. When you're clearly trying to empathise with the mourner's personal experience, you can bring an enormous amount of comfort. But empathy is not simply about comparing it to your own experience. Mum's old nanny constantly talked to us about her dying elderly brother. Frankly it doesn't really compare and it was anything but helpful.

I did a lot of crying in my bedroom. We had an old nanny we called Bessie who told me at one point, 'The crying's got to stop you know, you can't grieve for ever.' That was not particularly helpful.

What Helped – and What Didn't?

My sister and I weren't really allowed to help with the funeral. It just wasn't an option. We were seen as children, and were expected to go back home and slot in to our allocated roles. So I didn't find any aspect of this stage cathartic.

I hated the funeral. It was really difficult. It was a Catholic service held in a horrid, cold church. I felt completely overwhelmed looking after my parents. I remember all of us holding each other up. I held Papa and my sister held Mum. That was generally the configuration in our family. The church was full, but I don't remember 'seeing' people. In the car after the service, on the way to the burial, I broke down. Mum snapped and said, 'Can you be quiet? You're disturbing Papa's driving.' I stopped immediately. I was protecting my parents again.

A week after the funeral we held a Requiem Mass for Duncan, and afterwards I met some friends at the local pub. It was a strangely jolly gathering, but again, practically no one referred to the service or my brother. Indeed, the only person who did so was my friend Liam. He was very sweet to my mum too, by acknowledging it with her, and he'd also made a point of putting his arm around her as we walked into the church. Only afterwards did I realise why – it was because he knew! He had lost his mother when he was only sixteen; he knew instinctively how important it was for the friends of the bereaved to cross that 'line of death' and say or do something that acknowledges and brings it into reality. The fact that Liam was so considerate of my mother meant more to me than him being there for me. I was grateful that he felt able to talk to her about her sadness, and she definitely appreciated his recognition. Any act of consolation, however small, is worth its weight in gold, and remembered long after the event.

I didn't broach the subject of Duncan with my other friends because I didn't want to embarrass them. If they felt they couldn't say anything, then it was clearly difficult, and I didn't want to make it harder for them by bringing it up, so it remained the elephant in the room. And I think I didn't want to be different from them either; it was almost a relief to be 'normal' for a while. Also, I somehow felt responsible for them – if it hadn't been for me, they wouldn't have had to be there.

You become quite self-obsessed at times like these. At least I did, and it felt as if everything was down to me. A bit like a child who feels that everything is their fault. I guess I would have been grateful if someone had eased that sense of burden in some way. I would have liked it if people around me were ready to listen, without wanting to 'fix it' – just reassuring me it was OK to talk about it.

When Duncan died Matthew was working 100-hour weeks as a junior doctor, so he simply wasn't able to be around very much. Although this was something I'd got used to and had come to expect, he was still a strong presence at the funeral, and I remember being comforted by the fact that he was crying. Not many of my friends were in serious relationships at that time, while I'd already been with Matthew for four years, so I wonder whether a lot of them thought I'd be fine because I had him. I had two or three close friends who were sort of hovering and I guess that felt enough at the time. Perhaps I'd have felt my other friends' presence more if they hadn't relied on my relationship holding me up – especially given that, in the event, his work meant he wasn't able to provide much support. So I'd say it's best not to presume that someone is OK just because they are in a relationship.

Communication was so different then, too. You couldn't text or send messages on Facebook. So in a way we were used to *not* being in touch with people. And I think that gave people more room to hide from the bereaved: out of sight, out of mind.

Another thing that was different then was the amount of outside support available – no one thought that my sister and I might need some therapy or help as bereaved siblings. We just had to get on with it. I think it's important to remember the siblings, and that they are suffering too.

People seem to want a role when it comes to supporting the bereaved. Susan, our neighbour and closest family friend, took on the role of social secretary, updating people on how we were all coping. I think there can be an unspoken who's-helping-out-the-most competition, whereby some people want to 'help' and be centre stage, but that's not always useful and it can push others away.

I went back to work quite soon after Duncan died. Work didn't really allow for much talking about what had happened, so I just got on with it. I went out a lot with people from work, which was a distraction, a bit of escapism, maybe. These friends were temporary, but it felt easier to be around different people. There was one person at work who was really helpful. He was older, wiser and a bit removed – he was my 'separate person', purely my support. I was able to talk to him about Duncan and that was a major help, actually.

What I wanted from people was quite simple; it was just hard for them to give it. People often think they have to 'fix it', but they know they can't, so then they don't do anything. Just really be there, and don't be afraid. Tiny things can mean a lot: a little gift or just a gentle enquiry about how the bereaved person is.

And Lastly …

Don't think, 'I mustn't bother that person'. I've thought that before and I have to remind myself that it's not about me. Have the courage to care for the person in mourning, in even the smallest way. Use your wisdom. Everyone knows what to do deep down; they just don't always take time to think about it. It's when you revert to thinking about yourself that you make mistakes – by thinking, 'Oh, I haven't done enough' or by doing too much and overcompensating. Take a moment to think about the person, your friend, about who they were when they were not bereaved, and then you will feel more confident about what is best for them.

What you can learn from Nicola's story

A couple of people have talked of wanting to be surrounded by normality and everyday activity. I certainly did. But Nicola gives us an alternative perspective. The idea of vacuuming didn't sit right with her at all, and it wouldn't for many others I'm sure. She liked the celebratory feel of each evening in the run up to the funeral, the sense that the event of the death was still being marked in some way. So be mindful of this with your friend – which would they prefer?

Also, in contrast to Rose (see page 48), Nicola found great comfort in having friends who were showing support for her mother. It somehow lifted the burden from her, so try and gauge which would be right for your friend. I guess that it depends very much on what other support is available to them, so look around and think how best you can 'slot in'.

However, if your friend, like Nicola, has a natural tendency to turn inwards to draw on their own strength, remind them what's available outside, too. They probably won't take you up on the offer, but knowing it is there is just as important.

Chapter 9

Anna, whose son died

My husband, Roger, and I had always had this rainy-day project to build a boat. When we moved to Cape Town in South Africa we knew it was the perfect time. Roger, my daughter, Hannah, and I set up there and began building a life – and a 105-foot racing boat. Eighteen months later I was pregnant with Joe. Although Roger and I started having marital problems shortly after he was born, Joe had a lovely and blissful time, with a great big garden to play in, a swimming pool and was constantly surrounded by people who loved him and looked after him.

It had never crossed my mind that I wouldn't have children, but when Joe was born I was nevertheless struck by how lucky I felt to have him. Everyone who came to visit me said the same. It felt special. I was 30 years old and I had a girl and a boy, and they were perfect and healthy. But there was something so precious about Joe that I just knew he was only passing through, that somehow he wouldn't last. I used to get up in the middle of the night and go to his cot to check he was still there. It wasn't in a neurotic way – it was almost like sleep-walking – and, strange as it may seem, I never felt afraid of the fact that he wouldn't always be there. I'd often tell my mum to come over and see him because he wouldn't be around for ever.

In my mind I had envisaged finding his cot empty. There was no outward hysteria in these fantasies (or whatever they were) – just silent screaming. The reality was, of course, completely different. Despite my forebodings, I initially felt cheated, robbed of my child, very cross and hurt. And that it was the wrong time, too soon. I felt all the natural things that everyone else would feel; it was just that there had been this anticipation there before.

The four of us had left Cape Town for the weekend to go and see an exceptional horticultural phenomenon called the 'Flower Carpet' by the river. During the day the heat was extraordinary and at night the temperature plummeted to zero. The air con in our hotel room doubled as a heater, and although we noticed an odd smell when we turned it on – rather like old dust drying on a heater element – we lingered long enough that we became accustomed to it. Then, once Joe was asleep, I nipped out briefly to join Roger and Hannah and give my order for supper.

In fact, the smell was coming from the plug in the wall behind our beds and this was heating up and melting the foam mattresses. By the time I returned to the room, columns of black smoke were coming out of the vents above the door. I rushed back to the refectory and screamed at Roger that our room was on fire and together we ran straight back. But in opening the door, we let oxygen in and the room burst into flames. We grabbed Joe from the cot and ran outside. In the eight minutes that I was gone from the room Joe had inhaled enough poison to kill him.

Someone nearby happened to be a doctor. He tried to resuscitate Joe, but told me straight away that there was a very good chance that it wasn't going to work, and that after a certain amount of time it's often better the person doesn't come back – that Joe's brain wouldn't be the same. We tried for a while, on our way to the hospital, but eventually the doctor suggested we stop, and he pronounced him dead.

All I wanted was to go home with Joe, but the nurse at the hospital wouldn't let me; she said Joe would have to go into the morgue for the night. I refused and there was a stand-off – the nurse kept trying to take Joe from me, and I was very protective and aggressive. She seemed to be so vindictive and I couldn't understand why. She eventually she told me her eighteen-year-old son had died two months before and she hadn't been allowed to take him home. Then she burst into tears and let me go.

I felt very self-conscious walking back in the very bright light of the enormous full moon, holding my dead baby. We were moved to a bungalow and I put Joe on the chaise longue at the end of the bed for the night. It was really important to me that he was with us.

What Does It Feel Like?

There are two sides to my feelings about Joe's death. On the one hand, twenty-two months is not a life, and I felt really indignant that this precious little person should have had to suffocate in smoke and be taken from us so soon. I was also really angry about the timing because Roger and I had just started trying to rebuild our relationship after a very difficult time. This compounded my indignation: even though I'd felt it was somehow always going to happen, I didn't understand why then. Why was this happening when everything was beginning to go right? I was also angry with Roger. He'd missed all that time and now Joe was dead, and the two of us were quite separate in our ways of coping. I didn't feel any sense of togetherness at all.

But on the other hand, Joe was totally undamaged. He was dead, but perfect. And I was incredibly grateful for that. Had he died in a car crash, it would have been different. I feel very supported by that, and lucky that he had a really beautiful life, surrounded by people who adored him. I feel content to think of the nourishment and love in his life.

I also had a religious structure because I was brought up Catholic, so there were some rules that I felt I had to adhere to. I rang our church, even though it was 600 miles away, as I thought the priest would tell me what to do. I was grateful that with the chaos of emotions going on in my head this gave me some parameters, some boundaries.

I was surprised by my reaction. I had always felt that Joe would not last for long, but I never imagined that I would cope so silently. I wanted the world to stand still. Everyone appeared to be going around like nothing had happened. I wanted to shout out, 'Hang on a minute! Something really essential has happened!'

For months I'd think Joe was back. I'd hear his little footsteps around the house, and call out, 'Hi!' Then I'd go into his room looking for him. I realised quite soon that I just had to let those memories wear out.

I was so far away from familiar friends and family, and had been for so long, that I was used to that sense of distance. I can imagine that if I'd been in England, bumping into people asking how I was all the time, it would have been very different.

I called my parents the night Joe died. Jill, who had worked for my family my whole life, answered the phone. My parents were asleep, so I asked her to tell them for me. The first thing she said was, 'Oh my God, your mum said you knew this would happen.' I knew then that Mum had taken it on board and that was consoling. My parents got on the first available flight and I collected them from the airport the next day.

What Can You Say – and Avoid Saying?

The following day, before taking Joe to the morgue, I went to see Father Michael, the priest. I placed him on the altar and said, very angrily, 'There you are, God. You've taken my child, what are you going to do about it?' I was furious. 'You're quite lucky, actually', Father Michael replied. He said we should remember we still had Hannah and that tomorrow would be a day like any other for her – she would want to go to school, see her friends and go to after-school activities and so on. 'You have an in-built structure that you have to follow, whether you want to or not.' He was right – life would carry on, despite what we felt at the time, but he needn't have said it right then, and I did not like hearing it.

As soon as my parents arrived, I took them straight to the morgue, so they could see Joe. While Mum was in with him, my dad turned to me and said, 'Darling, don't imagine you're going to have children again.' I remember thinking that nothing could have been further from my mind, and I hated that he thought I might want to replace Joe. I was really shocked at first. I could-n't think about tomorrow or the next week, let alone another child. I was far too wrapped up in the emotions of the moment and all I wanted to do was wallow in how I was feeling. Little did we know then that almost nine months later I would give birth to another child.

A mutual friend told Roger, in front of me one evening, that 71 per cent of marriages break down after the death of a child. This was the worst thing anyone said. Roger then reinforced it another evening, saying: 'Do you know, the stats are really stacked against us ... we're probably going to break up.' I was livid. We'd virtually broken up anyway, but the last thing I wanted was to hear stats about the impact of Joe's death.

I remember lots of women asking if I'd been to see a counsellor. I think this was because I talked a lot about Joe, and what it was like to have lost him, and some people found that really uncomfortable, especially as I didn't cry very much when I spoke about it. It seemed their only offer of consolation was to tell me to go and talk to someone else about it in case I wasn't dealing with it as well as I thought I was. In the end I did go and see someone because I worried I was missing a trick and would end up in a madhouse a few months down the line.

We received many extraordinary letters from friends and family but I was brutally aware of their awkwardness, their inability to know what it might feel like, but clearly knowing that words had to be scribbled and something had to be acknowledged. Again and again I heard from people who imagined that had we been in the UK we might have been able to save him. *If only ...*

Some letters were such a recipe though, but the problem with words is that you dip in and out of moods and that affects what you need. So some days you'll get a really well thought-out letter from a friend, imagining what it must be like, and you will feel grateful for the time they've spent thinking about you. And then other days, you may be feeling angry and indignant, and that same letter will make you feel hurt that they have pried so deeply into what you're going through. You're more alive somehow, so you see and feel things more keenly; you're vulnerable and open to every possible feeling. And that's the tricky thing for friends. Ultimately though, it is always better to send a letter, and get it wrong, than not to write at all.

What Helped – and What Didn't?

When I got back from the hospital, the doctor who had been at the scene told me very firmly that I had to call someone immediately. I didn't want to and couldn't understand why he was so insistent. He said that the next day I would wake up and feel very alone: 'You have got to call someone and tell them, "This has happened to me",' he said. Eventually, I agreed to let him ring a friend of ours who drove from Cape Town to where we were. I will forever be grateful to him for that.

I was so grateful when Emma, a girl I had met since we'd been living in South Africa, turned up the day we got back to Cape Town. She said that she would be there every day to answer the phone and speak to the police for us. She insisted that I would need her help and that although she knew I wouldn't want it or understand why it was necessary, she was going to stay regardless. She was right. The police spoke very little English, and were so persistent. She was there from nine to five every day to help. It was really amazing.

We planned a little funeral for Joe, and he lay at the end of our bed the night before. The boys in the boat yard made us a small coffin and it was a rather lovely, collaborative community thing. I wanted the coffin to be open. That seems odd now, but he was still so very perfect and I wanted to commit every bone, scar and freckle to memory. I also thought it would be helpful for Hannah to be able to explain to her friends. She helped me paint the coffin and place flowers around him. It also felt important to me for everyone else to see him. Because he was little and so precious and innocent, it somehow seemed appropriate. I wanted it to be a visceral and visual thing that no one put the lid on.

I really didn't want many people around after Joe died. I had my parents there and there was enough going on with Roger that I didn't need anyone else. As it turned out though, the house was full most of the time, not only with my parents and Emma, the self-appointed 'police-liaison' friend, but also a live-in priest!

Weeks before Joe died, there had been an announcement that Father Michael was going on holiday and that the visiting priest would need somewhere to stay. I'd offered to host him, and it was only after Joe died that I remembered the Irish Catholic priest was about to move in. I hadn't asked Roger, but he told me he felt really great about it. He was such a blessing; he had an amazing presence and he and Roger had lots of chats. I was pleased for Roger about this, as I think he had felt quite excluded, especially as my parents were there, too.

I felt lucky to have my parents around. My mum was good with Hannah and Dad was good with all the post-death admin, although he was quite clinical in his approach, which I found a bit difficult. But it was hard to see their grief. I was so self-absorbed and it hadn't occurred to me that this was also their loss.

I found that in South Africa there was an ease around death that contrasted with attitudes in the West. There, they seemed to live life in the knowledge that their days are numbered, thankful for each day and every child and not expecting that there will always be a hospital, a pill or a doctor to somehow save them from the pain and reality of death. This helped to give me an understanding that death doesn't have to be the end of the world; obviously it's not a great thing, but it is inevitable.

I got a phone call from a woman who ran a counselling service, offering group therapy and the opportunity to talk to someone else who had lost a child. I declined – I'm not sure why. It might have been a pride thing, and the fact that I'm not a girls' group kind of person; or maybe I wasn't feeling brave enough. But the other mother rang me anyway and told me how she had lost both her children through a drowning accident in a pool. I was so humbled – she had had such a horrific experience and yet she was fine to talk about it. It didn't make me want to go to any of the groups, but I was grateful, seeing for the first time that my life could have been so much worse.

I used to imagine that one day I would wake up and understand why we had to have this experience, that it would lead me to some new path, place, knowledge. I am still waiting for the 'reason why'. But I am grateful it has enabled me to talk very easily about the loss of a child and I appreciate it when the space to talk openly and frankly is available and when people are able to listen without awkwardness.

And Lastly ...

It is twenty-four years since Joe died. Emma, the girl who came for four days still sends me a message every year telling me she thinks of me. That is amazing.

Prayer was also very powerful. I really felt it. Even meditation – whether religious or non-religious – can be a hugely underestimated tool for both the bereaved and non-bereaved. Since time immemorial, communal prayer has been a gentle support for people – a coming together and concentration of the mind and thought. That feeling of being part of a chain, joined together in sympathy and thought, and that moment of reflection and taking time out to empathise with others and know that we are all part of a very joint effort can be enormously consoling.

What you can learn from Anna's story

Anna says some things that I imagine may shock a lot of people, especially parents. Not only does she tell us she somehow knew her son was going to die, but she also talks openly about coming to accept his death. If you experience something similar, while it may sit a little uncomfortably with you, try not to judge and try and bear it. After all, it won't be nearly as uncomfortable as the underlying pain of their loss. While she coped with strength, and mostly alone, she also referred a number of times to wanting to wallow and wanting it to be all about Joe's loss.

I think we can also learn something about confidence. Just as the doctor told Anna to call someone, if you feel you know something will almost certainly help your friend, tell them. And don't be afraid to be insistent. Sometimes a healthy dose of gusto is just the ticket.

Finally, if you live in a different country to your loved one who has just been bereaved, take the distance into account. There will be a number of implications, not least cultural differences. Anna says she was helped to understand that death doesn't have to be the end of the world. But knowing that death is understood and responded to very differently in her native country may well have left her feeling isolated and detached from old friends. Take a moment to consider their location and how this may impact what they need from you from afar and their capacity to receive it.

Chapter 10

Yvonne, whose daughter died

My daughter Helen died aged forty-five in 2013. We were exceptionally close and had a very loving and physically warm relationship.

Helen had been depressed for a few years, following a failed business venture and relationship and, as a result, was drinking too much. She always seemed to be functioning well enough, but eventually she was rushed to hospital and ended up in intensive care for five weeks. Her liver and kidneys were damaged and she was on breathing apparatus, dialysis and liver support. The prognosis suggested that she could recover, but she never made it home. Her death came as a complete shock to me, the family and the hospital staff.

Helen was only semi-conscious for much of the time she was in hospital. Occasionally we'd laugh together, but conversations were generally one-way. The whole family – her sister, Audrey, her children, her children's father and I – had a rota between us, so that she was never alone. I never thought for one second that she would die. I was simply waiting for her to come home. At one point the nurse said, 'This is your room, Helen; you must have everything you want here – pictures, photos, ornaments ... ' Now, looking back I think that was quite telling. But even her daughters, Lily and Diana, seemed quite relaxed.

Eventually, Helen got too weak for dialysis, and had lost control over her bowels. I hadn't left her for weeks, but I had a hospital appointment I had to attend in London, so I asked the ward sister if she thought I could go back for one night. She assured me it was fine, and said I could stay for a few nights if I wanted – nothing was going to happen. I saw Helen at lunchtime. Both the girls were there, sitting on her bed, with David, their dad. I stood at the end of the bed and told her I was off for one night and I'd be back the next day. I didn't give her a hug because I didn't want everyone to move, so I just blew her a kiss and she blew one back. At about 3 a.m. the phone rang. It was Audrey and she told me Helen had died.

Helen's eldest daughter, Diana, had stayed with her the night she died. The night staff didn't know her as well as the day staff and there were only two nurses on duty. Apparently, Diana woke in the night to find Helen couldn't breathe. The nurses did as they had done previously and suctioned the liquid from her lungs, but half an hour later she couldn't breathe again. This time the nurses just told her to cough. Then Audrey arrived. When it was clear that Helen really wasn't breathing, they pulled out all the stops, but by this time she'd had a heart attack from the lack of oxygen. Then she died.

I think I knew as soon as the phone rang. I said, 'I'll come right away', and then I rushed into my bedroom and yelled out to my partner, Bob: 'It's Helen!' I cried immediately. It was a kind of terrible explosion and I was in an absolute panic about getting there. Bob rushed up, got his clothes on and called a taxi – we both knew there was no way I could wait on a station platform for an hour, or sit on a train or buy tickets. I just knew that I had to get there – even though I was too late. That's quite strange, I suppose. I could have thought to myself, There's nothing I can do. But instead I tried desperately to get there as soon as I could – almost as if she was still alive. I think I thought I could somehow make it unreal once I was there.

It was the strangest journey I've ever made. I cried the whole time, completely oblivious to the fact that I was in somebody else's car – that there was this stranger driving us somewhere. He didn't really exist.

We got to the hospital at about 7a.m., just as the day staff arrived. They were all in complete shock and sat and wept with us. They were so distressed and kept apologising to me for telling me I could go home. I really didn't feel any blame towards the day staff. It was the night staff I was unsure about.

They asked if I wanted to see Helen. In a way I wish I hadn't. She had looked so ill for so long, yet now she looked amazing – like she did before she was ill so it felt even more impossible to believe she was dead. I wanted to hold her, but then I couldn't because I knew she'd be cold. I couldn't bear that.

What Does It Feel Like?

Mostly, I've been in complete disbelief. I've often said to myself, 'This isn't true . . . she can't have gone.' It's one of the reasons I haven't been able to go to her grave yet. It feels too finite – too real. And I feel like a failure. A part of me feels I should have been there to hold her in my arms when she died. But I also think I might have panicked. Mostly, I feel I failed because I was aware for two years that she was drinking too much. Everyone was. But we all kept saying there was nothing we could do – we couldn't force her to stop drinking. But I think I was very selfish, actually. I was scared she'd get cross and upset with me if I approached her about it. I wish I had taken the risk.

Audrey and I have a tricky relationship, but when Helen died we knew we had to co-operate with each other. The truth is that I was closer to Helen. We did far more together, partly because Audrey had a big family with five children, but also because we just got on well. We shared the same sense of humour. I did treat Helen differently, for all kinds of reasons, but in large part because she expressed her need for me more than Audrey did.

It is strange how you can keep going in such a different world – between death and the funeral. It becomes something you want to do well; you want to please so many people, including the dead person. But this experience felt so different to previous losses. This is a grief that I didn't know existed. It's like the whole bottom of my life has fallen away for cvcr.

I didn't feel there was much allowance made for the fact my loss was so great. One of Audrey's daughters paid lip service to it, but on the whole, most of my family seemed unable to actually put themselves in my shoes. Of course, I didn't expect Helen's daughters to empathise with me because their own loss was so enormous, but they did. Otherwise, I felt my grief was only acknowledged as being different by my friends and my partner. I was a bit baffled by that. I would have expected a wee bit more.

I basically just needed understanding and caring people around me. Bob has been absolutely amazing, in just saying, 'Of course this is how you feel; this is the greatest loss … ' He suffers from depression and sometimes he says, 'I'm sorry I can't be there the way I want to be', but it doesn't stop him putting his arm around me and that's all I need. Of course, I do sometimes feel it's a bit much for him to have to be with me, but he's great and I can't help but use his support. I don't choose to talk to him, or to weep. It just happens.

What Can You Say – and Avoid Saying?

The first place I went after seeing Helen in the hospital after she'd died was to Audrey's. We were drinking tea in her sitting room and I started to cry. I think I called out to Helen, 'I want you back', and Audrey told me to stop. She said that I was impeding Helen on her next journey. I was horrified to hear that in that moment, and I don't know what I said back, but whatever it was absolutely riled her and she told me leave immediately after that. I often have to remind myself that Audrey had held her dying sister in her arms only a few hours before. She also has a completely different set of beliefs to me and for her, moving on to the next phase of life was what was important.

All my friends have made themselves present to me both physically and with their words, telling me how much they cared about Helen or just putting an arm around me and saying, 'Are you OK, Yvonne?' Asking in such a way, with a physical act of consolation, somehow makes room for me not to be OK, so that I know I can say, 'No'. I have made very close new friends because of Helen dying.

One particularly wonderful woman called Rebecca, who I met at my church – she knows exactly. She'll simply say, 'Of course you're not OK. How could you be?' Another friend of mine, Sue, has said, 'Yvonne, of course life will never be the same for you', and that's the sort of acknowledgement I need. Other people have said it will get easier, and I know it will on one level, but in another way it won't. Maybe I'll get on with my life more, but it'll never be easy to not have Helen.

One friend has taken on the role of helping me get to and from places. She rings to offer a lift, saying, matter of factly, that she will collect me. She's a very practical person and doesn't say much or show a lot of emotion, but she's been fantastic. Even though she works full-time and is incredibly busy she'll just say, 'Come over, I'll cook you supper'. She's always specific about when I should go, and I also know that she wouldn't say yes to anything if it wasn't right for her.

Some people find it too difficult to handle though. I only had one friend who said something that really hurt me. She told me Helen wouldn't want me being upset like I was. I was so cross; I told her that she was wrong, and in fact Helen would be pretty pissed off if I wasn't upset. She obviously couldn't cope and it made me realise that we were not as close as I had thought.

The first time I went to the dentist after Helen died I told him about what had happened and he proceeded to tell me all about his dying mother. I thought it was extraordinary. I guess that was how he coped. He's a nice man, and I suppose he was trying to share the experience with me, but I did mind that he was trying to be 'in the same boat' as me. I couldn't understand why he was comparing his mother's illness to my loss.

That has happened with other people too. Somebody I know quite well whose sister died a few months after Helen, rang me and said how awful she was feeling, what a shock it had been and how difficult she was finding it to cope. Eventually, I interrupted her and said, 'I do know what it's like', and she said, 'Oh yes, how awful for you too. You must know.' The truth is, I didn't agree that we were feeling the same; of course, losing a sister is dreadful, but it's not the same.

What Helped – and What Didn't?

The whole family wanted Helen to be buried. Her daughter Diana was passionate about finding the perfect place to bury her, so we spent a lot of time looking. Eventually, we found a place – it was very near to where we lived, near Helen's infant school and I knew the church there well. Helen had wanted a cardboard coffin and Audrey took it home to decorate. She and her children and Lily and Diana spent three evenings painting it. She said I was welcome to join them, but I just couldn't possibly do it. They covered the coffin in the most beautiful designs, with flowers, Helen's name, hearts ... It was amazing, what they did. When I saw it in the church, I was blown away. It was stunning.

Helen's friends were wonderful at the funeral. To my astonishment the church was filled with well over a hundred people – school friends she hadn't seen for twenty years, teachers, old boyfriends, people who'd travelled from all over the world to be there. Helen had very low self-esteem, so I wished she'd been able to see how loved and valued she was.

The people I've had the most help from are from the church I go to. It's not a run-of-the-mill church – it attracts people who are alternative thinkers and rescues a lot of people who've been through horrendous experiences. From the word go, two or three people there could sense when I just needed an arm around my shoulder. Early on, two people asked me out for lunch a few times. Another friend has got tickets for the theatre. And Zoe, a close friend, but one who I don't see very often, has arranged to meet me for a meal a couple of times. My closest friend, who has lost her husband, took me out a lot at the beginning too. All these activities and indulgences have been a great way for my friends to support me. Not only do they take my mind off the agony, but they also show an awareness of what I might need in that moment.

Karen, my step-daughter wasn't able to come and visit Helen in the hospital and instead of ringing me for updates, she phoned Bob every day. If I'd wanted her to ring me she would have, but she had the sensitivity to call Bob, so that I didn't have to constantly retell the story. She lost her husband not long before Helen died. Her loss is so enormous – her husband's absence is different from Helen's because Helen wasn't there with me every day. Karen and I have been able to share that and talk about the differences. That has been enormously comforting.

Not everyone has had the same sensitivity. After Audrey insisted I leave I didn't know where to go so I asked a friend who lived near her, as I knew she was going away a few days later. Bob and I would only be in their way for a couple of days and then I hoped we could house-sit for them. She said, 'I suppose so', which wasn't exactly the most enthusiastic response. Then, just before she was due to go away she told us we had to leave. I was so hurt and I'm still finding it difficult to forgive her. While I understand we were probably not the best company, to be messed around like that felt unbearable. Consistency is very important. Don't offer something you can't follow through with.

I think it's really important to consider how well you know the bereaved person before taking action. Someone once came up to me whom I didn't know very well at all, and she didn't know about Helen. In a strange way, it wasn't difficult to tell her because she's not a close friend, so it was all relatively matter of fact. She said how sorry she was, but then she kept on at me, asking questions about how it happened, how I was feeling and so on. And I just didn't want to talk to her about it. I felt she was clinging to me for longer than she would otherwise have done and that made me feel uncomfortable. I just wanted her to go away. If you don't know a person very well, don't latch on to them just because they've told you something terrible.

Letters were a great comfort, but I was irritated by people

who said, 'I would have written, but I didn't know your address.' This was the case with one woman who could easily have found out my address had she tried, so I felt very alienated from her after that. I wasn't able to connect with someone who couldn't be bothered to write or call or anything.

It is really wonderful knowing I can just go to my church and sit in a corner and know that there are a few people who will get it right. Experiencing the silence within the service was often very emotional and I preferred either to leave immediately afterwards, evading conversation with anyone, or to find a spot at the rear of the church, where I could stay in that peaceful and emotional moment. I didn't really want comfort from anyone. Most people respect this. I think it is about me trying to avoid my own distress.

A need to escape has been a prominent aspect of my experience of grief. I tend to avoid phone calls and prefer texting, as it gives me time to prepare and get away if I need to. I haven't wanted people at my flat much either. And I feel a real need to be able to leave places when I want to leave. I went to a barn dance with some very close friends and knew as soon as I walked in that I couldn't possibly stay. I had to get out of there, quickly. But the friend I was staying with lived miles away, so I was trapped. I told another friend and she immediately took me up to a balcony and sat me down. I told her not to stay and she didn't push it, which I really appreciated. Another time, I was looking forward to a big party, but an hour before I was due to go, I just knew I couldn't go through with it. Sometimes those kind of celebratory distractions are not what you want. And that really needs to be OK with the people around you.

Sometimes though, being in an intense, sombre environment in which people expect you to talk about it can be just as panic-inducing. One of my oldest friends, Hilary, who knew Helen from when she was a little girl, has been so amazing; but she's almost got it *too* right, to the extent that I haven't called on her or taken her up on a lot of her offers. She's a great person and I care for her more than any other friend, but she can almost be too understanding sometimes. It isn't what she says – she says very little – but she'll just come and sit by me, put her arm around me or stroke my hair and sometimes it's overwhelming. She can see too much of the pain and so there's no escape. If I go out for a meal with another friend, there will be a supportive element to it, but there will also be some frivolity, so it will be a distraction, which is sometimes just what I need.

Being around other people who have experienced loss is also a tricky one; it varies so much, depending on the person, their loss and how they deal with it. Karen and I can discuss our bereavements very naturally. If she talks about Mike, it is not like it was with my friend who called about her sister. But another woman who lost her son often tries to share the pain, and although we have both experienced the loss of a child her feelings don't resonate with me. Because rightly or wrongly, it seems to me that whatever she's feeling, it cannot be as bad as what I am feeling. It's dreadful I know, but that's what feels true for me.

And Lastly . . .

Accept that you don't know how it feels. One of the best things to say is: 'I can't possibly understand how dreadful this must be for you.' That is the opposite of someone saying they know how you feel, and that really matters. When it's the loss of a child I also think the acknowledgement that it's a totally unnatural state of affairs is important.

What you can learn from Yvonne's story

I believe that losing a child is the greatest loss. Many people would agree. If you do too, don't be afraid to acknowledge it. Yvonne also talks a lot about comparative grief. Be careful with how much you share your own experiences. Quite often people need their loss to be a totally unique experience.

Also, remember that bereaved people are often incredibly fickle, especially in the early days. Be prepared for a sudden change of heart in all circumstances. If you organise a trip away for them, don't be cross if they tell you they want to go home as soon as they've landed in the sunny destination!

And finally, even if you feel confident and comfortable talking about the gritty, dark stuff, like Yvonne's friend Hilary, be careful you don't set yourself up as being associated solely with this type of support. Sometimes the bereaved person will not want to be seen with all their raw and ugly grief, and so they might end up avoiding you during the times they want it to be invisible or when they feel like being less serious. This could have a more permanent bearing on your friendship and you might find it harder to reconnect once your friend has worked through the hardest phases of the grieving process.

Chapter 11

Stewart, whose father died

My relationship with my father was nice but distant – so distant it was quite amusing. His name for me was 'boy' and, after about the age of twelve, I didn't call him anything. We were both members of a great club and when I went there for lunch with a colleague, in a room half the size of a tennis court, he would often be there too with his own lunch companion. We'd look over from our respective tables and just raise an eyebrow at each other. We both enjoyed it and didn't feel the need to display anything more; we thought we were being quite cool. Then we would talk on the phone a few days later and each ask who the other had been with. But in fact, there was a lot of emotion and warmth underneath all that. It was just this absurd Edwardian notion that it was better to hide our feelings.

Five years ago, while on the Tube going to work, he had a massive heart attack. The train was running through Warren Street Station, near a big London hospital, so there happened to be lots of doctors on board. He was incredibly well looked after and had the most amazing treatment on the train from three top doctors who tried to resuscitate him, but could not. The comforting thing about that was there was never the sense that anything more could have been done. The body was taken to hospital where my father was pronounced dead and then the police were informed. That is when things started getting complicated. At that point none of us knew what had happened, and the police couldn't find my mother, who is notoriously difficult to get hold of.

I saw my mother that evening, following the birth of my second son. We all met at St Thomas's hospital to see the new baby, expecting my father to turn up any minute. The baby's birth would have been the last bit of news he'd got from me. But he didn't come. My mum had an instinctive sense that something was wrong. She left the hospital worried, then later decided to go to the local police station where they told her he was dead. She waited until early the next morning before ringing to tell me the news. She just blurted it out and then started to cry on the phone.

By the time I got the phone call, some part of me had started worrying too, but it was still a shock. I kind of hollowed out. That was very quickly followed by a need to be efficient, to get on with things. My sister and I immediately clicked in to support roles and worked out what we had to do: go and see the body, inform people, think about the funeral, etc. Mum wasn't up to it, so that occupied us for the next few days. My mother and I also wrote a note of thanks to the doctors from the train and gave it to the police to pass on to them. I didn't ever want to meet them or know more. We knew there wasn't much more to tell, anyway; the police had been really good and told us the best story you could want to hear in the circumstances – that all the options were tried and nothing else could have been done.

What Does It Feel Like?

My son who was born that day got completely forgotten, and so did my partner, Jess. The bigger emotion was about the death and the birth took second place, which I know was unfair on Jess. It's psychologically interesting that the death was a bigger thing. It felt like the birth could be considered – celebrated – later; that this little blob would carry on growing and still be there months, years down the line. The death was somehow more immediate, important, overwhelming.

The juxtaposition of events was a huge source of interest for lots of people. My mother has this mystical idea that the two were linked; she feels that when one person is born it pushes someone else off the planet and the connection here was quite obvious. Personally, I think that it's coincidence, but it served as a graphic reminder of the cycle of birth and death that goes on all the time. I was instantly aware of the poetic possibilities which, indeed, I made more of in later years. This baby carried so much: my father's memory is – and always will be – connected to my son's birth; his birthday will always make me think of my father; and his middle name is taken after him. I knew instantly that this little chap was going to hold more than most of us, carrying forward my father's legacy, his spirit. The link between them both is very strong for me, but not in a mystical way. It's through memory, almost a literary connection, something one could write a story or poem about.

It was difficult for Jess. That was obviously when she needed a lot of attention and support from me, but we sort of divided things up and I dealt with my father and she dealt with the baby. I would definitely always tend to do things like this on my own in any case, and would have found it very hard to do it any other way. And as far as dealing with the baby was concerned, I wouldn't have been a great support in the best of circumstances; with our first baby I was very much in the background too and Jess's mum was the key supporter, so maybe there wasn't a huge difference. I guess we just played our roles as normal, and I didn't feel any pressure to be any other way. Jess and everyone just told me to look after my mum.

The interesting thing about my reaction was that I was quite angry with my father for dying. I didn't feel sad in a conventional way – I didn't cry – but I felt cross with him for going so prematurely, and that feeling remained with me throughout the first couple of years. It wasn't as simple as thinking he should have gone to the doctor or been more careful. It was more of a general 'fed-upness' with him and the universe for allowing this event to occur. It was unfair of him to die on us all. And annoying too. I'm aware that this could have been about wanting to get to know him better, but that doesn't resonate with me consciously. Another way of looking at it is that I've always felt angry with him for being a rather useless dad – if we ever asked him for advice, he would always make totally inappropriate suggestions as to what we should do or who we might ask to help us – and this somehow compounded that. So maybe it was residual anger: 'Here's another thing he's done that's useless.'

My sister didn't share this emotion. She was totally grief-stricken because for her he had been the parent who was most tender and protective – she'd lost the parent who she was closest to, whereas with me he had always been distant. But it was totally OK that we felt so differently about our loss. We left each other to it, and didn't need to talk about our respective feelings. In fact, we just don't talk feelings in our family either – we only talk plans.

I never actively wanted to share my experience with anyone. I did have moments of feeling upset or moved, and at those times, I'd have a wallow in my feelings, but it was always private. You wouldn't have noticed because there were never any outward signs. I'm naturally drawn to writing, so that's what I'd do – if anything – to channel my feelings. And I did write a lot.

I didn't want to communicate directly about it with anyone, but in some ways I wanted people to know via my written words.

What Can You Say – and Avoid Saying?

I wanted to carry on as normal. So that's what I tried to do. I had a conference in Barcelona a few days after my father died, and I didn't tell anyone what had happened. I just ran it as normal, and the way I did the job didn't seem to alter at all.

I really preferred it this way. Whether it's the best thing I can't say. But it fits with the whole attitude of keeping feelings hidden. I never wanted anyone to ask how I was feeling. People eventually started mentioning it, of course, but I'd always brush it off and say I was fine.

When I did have to tell someone, I would skate over the subject quite quickly, so as to avoid prompting any emotional response. And then I'd try not to get too involved in conversation with the person. But generally speaking, I didn't have a problem explaining what had happened or talking about how my mother was and so on. I can imagine that for some people retelling the story would be awful – another trauma in itself – but for me it was just a rather unpleasant duty. I did get irritated when I had to tell strangers about it – people at the phone company, for example. They'd say, 'Oh I'm so sorry,' and I'd often reply, 'Well, it's not the end of world; it's not unusual. You must have other customers who have died.' I know I wasn't particularly nice, and I'm sure I was unkind because underneath it all I was actually upset. There is probably nothing they could have said that in those moments that would have been right.

The key responses from my friends on hearing the news were: 'Sorry to hear', 'How did it happen?' 'Is your mum all right? 'Is there going to be a funeral?' I valued the fact that they followed protocol but knew not to say certain things. Instead they were able to signal them on a subconscious level, like, 'If you need me, ring me'. There was no real change – just life going on, so I had no sense of drifting from my friends.

I wrote the obituary for my father in *The Times* and was rather touchy about that because it was so personal. I put in some family jokes and made up a few things about what he had done because I knew that's what he'd have liked. My godmother's boyfriend was very critical of it and told my mother that sons should never write the obituary for their father. I thought it was quite inappropriate to say that. It was not what I wanted to hear and I was quite angry about it. I had enjoyed the experience.

I remember one good thing in particular that a friend said to me not long after my father died. When I bumped into him in the street one day I apologised for not having been in touch and told him the reason why. He looked at me with big, intense eyes and said, 'Oh, I'm so sorry for you. You will not feel normal for two years. Remember that.' And then he just rode off on his bicycle.

He turned out to be totally right – he really got it – and it gave me permission to feel weird. He was the first person to have said, essentially, that I had no power to do anything, which was very comforting because somewhere inside I had felt that there was a right way of grieving. But he made me feel like it wasn't up to me. We all put up so many barriers because we're insecure and don't want to display our frailties – especially me – so for someone to come along and blast through all those defences in one go was very comforting and a relief.

Of course, while it was great for me, saying a thing like that could also feel very intrusive to some people – not everyone wants to be told how long it will take. But the point is you're not trying to hit them with it; you just want to put it out there, so they can pick it up if they want to. You have to risk an unpleasant reaction sometimes in order to do anything or get anywhere.

What Helped – and What Didn't?

I probably thought I didn't need anything. And I didn't ask anything from anyone. There were absolutely no tears from myself or any of my family. And there were no hugs. I think some people cried at the funeral, but I don't remember very much about it. I had to speak and I remember going to the pub afterwards with a few people, but I didn't like that very much.

The church was another source of anger for me. Because my father was a weak presence in my life, I'd looked for replacements in figures of authority, such as older men and bishops. But I felt the church – like my father – had let me down, so the combination of being in a church and my father's funeral made me angry.

It all felt so meaningless. A lot of colleagues came along and then scuttled off straight away in a slightly useless way. Why come, I thought, if only to disappear immediately after? I think I wanted them to stay on some level. I know some people feel it's not appropriate for them to hang around at a funeral, but I think the right thing to do is to stay and try to communicate something to the bereaved. I know I would. I'd try and find somebody I know in the family and say something to them, perhaps check if I could do anything. Although I don't think this was what I needed, it was something I expected. It was a case of being critical of people for not living up to my expectations. Having said all that, I think that my mother and I were probably emanating mild disdain for everyone there, so no doubt they left for that reason. I'm sure most people's discomfort was a response to my own way of being.

Jess found and read a very emotional and revelatory piece I

wrote about my grief. I think it was nice for her to know how I was feeling considering I wasn't talking about it. I hadn't even told her I'd written it, but I was happy she knew. The piece was published, and although on the one hand I had a lot of hang-ups around it and avoided showing it to people, on some level I also really wanted them to read it. A lot of people did, and they liked it. Someone told me it reminded them of their own experience. I felt safer exposing my feelings in this way, at a safe distance. I guess it's a bit of a paradox: that I could have all these feelings and not want to tell anyone about them, but that I could write about them and put them 'out there' instead – because actually, perhaps I did want them to notice.

I didn't get any letters. My mother got lots and I think she liked that. I've always thought that sending a letter is one of the best things you can do. Those of my friends who knew my father all wrote to my mum and I was pleased about that.

Friends were much better than relatives at being there for me. I believe that friends are all that matter on the whole anyway. In fact, I think there should be a whole new social structure where families aren't important; they often only bring grief and unhappiness, so why bother? Fortunately, I consider my immediate family as part of my friendship group – in fact, my partner and my children are my best friends. My extended family, on the other hand, includes lots of people I don't like at all.

The best person in this group was Jess. I think what I really appreciated was just having someone around who was there when I needed them – but not expecting anything from me. What most people need is just someone there, just being there. It's an interesting concept of caring because it's not about trying to *do* anything, or 'fix it' – that tends to be more about the helper feeling useful. It's also not about probing or emotional digging. It's about just letting the other person have space, but still being present – getting on with your own activities, in the presence of the bereaved, like just doing your knitting in the corner while they sit and watch a film. It shows that you're willing to give up a load of other things you could be doing, and that you will just be there, unconditionally. Jess could have gone off to her parents or on holiday, but she didn't. She just stayed there, with me.

Some relationships have been strengthened as a result of my father's death. As I mentioned, I've always sought out father figures, and what probably happened is that I formed slightly stronger friendships with one or two of those people. Graham, aged eighty-three, is a very affectionate guy. We've always had a very warm relationship, but I see him much more now. Our friendship was somehow boosted by my father dying.

It's often surprising the characters who are there the most. The best relationship my mother established after my father died was with the man who ran the local corner shop. He was really kind to her and so sympathetic; she saw him every day and loved the support he provided by asking her how she was and acknowledging her loss.

And Lastly ...

I think this should be a rule, not just a tip: wait till things have calmed down, then go back, about a month later. Tell the person that you know it'll take a long time for it to feel OK again, and say: 'My position is I'm going to be around now, so regard me as being there if you're interested.' And then make sure you stick around. There's something amazing about the feeling in a bereavement that a friend is not going to go away. Of course, some people do forget, but it's worth trying to convey, as best you can, that you haven't.

I had an employee who died several years ago, and her mother has now just lost her husband. She's an old lady and very sweet and alone. Although I'm just the boss of her late daughter, I know I have a role to play in her bereavement, so in keeping with my rule, I'm going to call her in a month's time and tell her I'm coming for tea. Then I'm going to suggest that I organise something else for a month later. And then after that I'll arrange something again, maybe just once a year, the point being that I want to make it personal, physical and concrete.

What you can learn from Stewart's story

Try not to interpret your friend's reaction to the death. Stewart was angry after his father died. I interpreted his anger to be about the loss, but he understands it to be about the deeper and more hidden dynamics that existed in his relationship with his father. It might be about both, one or neither, but the important thing as friend and supporter is not to act out of your judgement. It needn't affect your ability to be there for them and support them in the way they need.

I think this story is really about respecting the bereaved's right to silence and privacy, while not ignoring the death. The scripted sayings such as 'sorry for your loss' and 'I'm thinking of your family' are there for a reason. Don't cut off all communication if your friend doesn't want to talk. Perhaps protocol has even more of an important function for those who seek help least. It allowed Stewart to know his grief was acknowledged, while not having to engage in heart-to-heart dialogue.

Chapter 12

Harry, whose father died

My father, Fred, took his own life when I was fourteen years old and my sister, Katie, was just a week away from her sixteenth birthday. He had spent his life battling manic depression, which finally got the better of him after multiple attempts at suicide throughout his adult life. In the end it was his illness that consumed him, although he did not live his life caged by it. He was an incredibly charismatic person, who helped people in both his role as a doctor and as a caring member of society.

Our parents separated when I was two, and my father remained an extremely loving parent who was there for both my sister and me. He hid his illness from us, and, for most of our lives, our mother agreed not to tell us what was going on either. But in our final year together everything began to unravel.

I was always rather star-struck by my father. Because I only knew him until I was fourteen, I never reached the real teenage parent-hating years; I think we'd probably have had a really terrible time if he'd lived beyond that. But instead, many of my memories are of me running around behind him, dressed up in suits to go to special events with him – being a mini Fred.

His manic highs and lows were normal to us. I thought everyone's dads were the same. We'd go and visit him in mental asylums and because he had quite a senior role in the health service he would tell us remarkable stories as to why he was there – because he knew too much, so they had to lock him away, for example. And that's what we believed.

We'd always know whether he was up or down within a second of seeing his face. I pride myself now in being able to read people because of that. I was very protective of my dad and, whether he was crying or overly happy, I always sensed I needed to help him. At the age of eleven I spent rather a lot of time desperately trying to calm him down. This sometimes meant convincing him not to make me bunk off school and take me home instead: 'Maybe we shouldn't fly to Brazil tomorrow, Dad – I have school.' That was what went wrong for me eventually – I wanted to help and protect him so much that I just couldn't handle it any more. I began seeing therapists and specialists, trying to figure out why I was so troubled and depressed.

When my dad saw the effect he was having on me he checked himself into a clinic. Then, when he came out, he announced to us that he was engaged to one of the other patients. He met us by the Millennium Dome in London to celebrate with champagne and was clearly on one of his highs. I knew instantly that something was brewing. Katie and I got in the car with him to go to see his sister, and as we drove along, he got increasingly erratic, crying one minute, then singing along to songs on the radio the next. He started talking nonsense about Brazil again, and suddenly, he just pulled over into a service station. He disappeared for about an hour and when he finally came back he threw me the car keys and told me to park up while he dragged Katie out of the car towards the shops. I was only thirteen and had no idea what to do, so I locked the car and went looking for them. As I got closer to the building I saw everyone staring at my dad. He had keeled over and was screaming about being diabetic. Eventually, the ambulance turned up. The crew were absolute bastards, saying spitefully, 'Your dad's not diabetic; he's not even ill'.

Dad kept talking nonsense all the way to hospital and said some horrible things to Katie about not wanting her and not loving her and he told me I was head of the family and needed to look after everyone. I knew then this was exactly why I had to keep myself together. Finally, my mum told us about dad's illness. I think I went into mental shutdown. I didn't truly accept it until after Dad died, and convinced myself Mum was lying. As a consequence, I chose to reject her and stay with my dad even more.

A few months after the car incident, I was pretty much living with Dad and had just started back at school. I fancied a girl in my Spanish class and I was friends with an old mate, Mike again. I felt good and everything seemed close to normal.

It was a Wednesday. Katie had to go back to Dad's to get her sports kit for the afternoon. Tuesday evenings were always at Dad's, so she'd been staying there the night before. She walked into the house and saw his legs hanging from the ceiling. Shortly after, I was called to the headmaster's office. I saw the chaplain and my mum and sister waiting in the room and I knew something was wrong immediately. My mum said, 'Your father's done something terrible. He's killed himself.' I felt stone cold.

What Does It Feel Like?

My initial reaction was one of calm. After being told the news I immediately comforted my mother and sister, stroking them and telling them that everything would be all right. I could hear Dad telling me to be responsible and to look after everyone.

The cold calm began to melt away over the next few days and I started to feel a stabbing pain in my chest with the realisation that I would never see my father again. I cried. I remember everything being so dark. It was the summer, so I know it was bright and sunny, but it just felt dark everywhere. I lay in my bedroom, sobbing, shouting, 'Why?!' Katie reacted in a similar way.

My depression escalated following Dad's death, but there was also a sense of relief that the thing I had unconsciously feared had finally happened. I felt guilt knowing that my difficulty in coping had pushed Dad further down into his own depression, and that guilt was borne out by his suicide note, which explained that he knew what a terrible effect his illness was having on me and that he couldn't bear it any more. But I also understood that in some way he saved me by his decision. At the time I only read enough of the note to make me feel responsible and sad, but I read it again more recently and realised just how much it was a product of the brain-bubbling conversation he used to have with himself. It is strange to have such an explicit explanation of his action, but knowing it was fuelled by a very different part of his brain, a part that wasn't able to deal with life and only made him react impulsively.

I had always felt more of a connection with older people, and my father's death made that rift with my peers greater still. My family had already been incredibly supportive in the lead-up to his death, particularly my mother, grandmother, godfather and his wife, and they continued to be so. They understood my need for distance at times and comfort when

I got too close to the edge. I didn't really know what I needed at the time – in fact, I don't think many people do. But by never being too forceful with the support or advice they gave, they allowed me to find my own way of comprehending what had happened and to figure out how I would cope and survive.

It was difficult dealing with the desire to blame someone for my father's death. Our 'fairy godmother', Lorna, who had looked after us every Tuesday, loved our dad like a son – he could do no wrong in her eyes, and she never saw his madness. Apparently, Dad told her what he was planning to do the night before he did it, and said his goodbyes. Although she may have had the opportunity to stop him, I think she just accepted his decision. Thankfully, I found that out quite a bit later, by which point she'd started going a bit dotty, and we felt able to forgive her because we knew how much she loved Dad.

Dad's doctor was not so easy to forgive, however. Her secretary told us that he'd called her the night before, or perhaps even on the night itself, and left a message for the doctor, which she had passed on to her, saying, 'I need your help, I'm scared I'm going to do something stupid'. The doctor had apparently said, in reference to my dad, 'Oh these fucking doctors; they're so arrogant, always telling us what to do.' We attempted to take this further, and my dad's friends helped for a bit, but we didn't go through with it. I don't think it would have been healthy for any of us. Dad loved the NHS really and to end all of his hard work like that wouldn't have done us any good.

What Can You Say – and Avoid Saying?

I called my best mate the day I found out and told him my dad had killed himself. He started laughing down the phone. It was horrible. But once he heard my sobbing he must have handed the phone immediately to his mum because the next voice I heard was hers, asking if I was OK. I told her what had happened and she just said, 'Oh Fred, what have you done?' She's very religious and I know the disappointment betrayed in her voice was to do with what she saw as my dad's failure to us, but all that was difficult to bear. That was the problem – I'd lost someone I loved, but it became about something else. I felt judged and hated that people judged my dad. He was dead. That should have been the point.

My cousin Isi, who is four years younger than me didn't know my dad well, but she took it really badly; mostly, because she knew I was so unhappy. She would cry and say, 'I feel so stupid being so sad, knowing everything you're going through', clearly thinking her own feelings paled into insignificance next to mine. Inevitably, I ended up supporting her and reassuring her that school and growing up are tough enough, and that she was allowed to feel sad too. And that was how I saw my role from then on: I had experienced something horrific, so I should now help others deal with their problems.

There was one girl at school, who I wasn't very close to, but who for some reason really seemed to want to be needed by me. She liked being in those situations, where she knew about people's private lives and could pass on the latest information to others. I remember feeling really great and happy at the wake after the funeral – the thing I'd been dreading was over, and everyone who was there loved my Dad. I was bouncing on the trampoline, when Holly came over and said, 'Harry, you're at your Dad's funeral, why are you so happy?' It completely knocked me for six and I think that was the last time we spoke. I was so hurt. She obviously didn't know how to deal with my facade – or maybe she just felt redundant if I was OK.

Religion plays a big role in this kind of death. Every single religious person advised me to turn to God, which drove me mad. I couldn't bear it when the local priest told me that my father's 'self-murder' may be condemned, but I could still be saved. The chaplain at my school was incredibly patronising too – the pity in his eyes when I was given the news left me feeling an intense anger towards him. I can understand that it's difficult bearing witness to a young person being told something of this weight, but I would have hoped he'd known better.

Anyone who said anything remotely against Dad made me angry. The vicar who ran the funeral ceremony implied that nothing could be done for Dad's soul. In fact, Dad had tried to engage with religion to help him through his illness. He referenced it a lot in his journals which show his desperation for some kind of help. It was sad that this source of support was now turning against him.

I remember having to talk to people about Dad and feeling afraid of how they'd react. I'd have to steel myself for their response in order to be able to cope. This made me wary of talking to people. Having to manage situations and question whether a forty-year-old could handle what I would tell them when I was only fourteen left me with something of a burden. I lost a huge amount of my childhood as a consequence and became a totally 'weird kid'.

Nowadays, I am prepared for when people ask me how my dad died. I pre-empt their awkward and often insensitive responses, and reassure them first that I am fine with what I am about to tell them: 'I'm totally OK with it; don't feel sorry for me, but . . . ' Once they know, I give them a choice of the A or B answer – the gory details or just the rough outline –

and they choose, depending on how much they think they can handle.

Family friends who reassured me that every year changes and that it won't necessarily get easier over time provided me with a lot of comfort. It meant that I felt allowed to take my time, and it helped me to accept that even if I found it easier to cope in one year, the next might be worse – the smallest thing could trigger an emotional setback. Anniversaries, birthdays, states of mind, anything can make you feel the same pain you did the day you lost someone.

What Helped – and What Didn't?

The funeral was amazing. I organised the music (an incredibly important part of my father's life), which was therapeutic in itself. I made a mixed tape to be played as we walked out of the church, the headline song being 'Dance the Night Away' by The Mavericks. It was also quite intense though. Almost everyone there felt responsible on some level – they all thought they should have been there for Dad more. And while so many of them wanted to make sure we were OK, we wanted them to know that Dad choosing to take his own life wasn't all desperate and tragic.

Many of Dad's close friends felt guilty and said they should have known, but my father always kept them at such a distance that they would never have been able to help him. My own experience of developing a facade has taught me a lot about relationships, and what it's like to reach out to someone who is hiding behind a mask. And my father's inability to turn to loved ones certainly helped me to realise the importance of asking for help in times of need – and also of being there for my loved ones. Now I have incredibly close relationships with my friends and family, who know immediately if I'm not myself.

One friend of my dad's felt so guilty he said he couldn't face coming to the funeral. He sent me a letter with a poem that I loved so much I read it out at the service. He had lost his wife and I understood that he could not handle such pain. However, I could not do the same in that situation – I would want to be there to comfort my friend's children. That relationship has not withstood the test of time and we are no longer in touch. But my father's friends who were with us during that time are still very much a part of my life.

My mum took a lot of time off which was amazing. She'd never done that before, as her business had always been her number-one priority, so that felt very special for us. My mum's mother really stepped up too. She looked after me, drove me around everywhere in her car, kept me well fed. Although she hated my dad, having seen what he did to her daughter and grandchildren, she was the one who gave the most love and support when it came down to it. I guess my other grandparents were dealing with the loss of their son.

My sister went back to school very soon after the funeral, to be distracted, but I hit rock bottom and didn't go back for months. I pushed a lot of people away and eventually told my mum I needed to be apart from her too. What did help was the support facility I got referred to – a day centre specifically for people who had experienced difficulties, ranging from bullying and abuse to bereavement. I cycled there three days a week and was surrounded by kids who were worse off than me. I was constantly supervised and gradually helped back into a routine.

Apart from my best friend and cousin, who spent as much time with me as they could, keeping me company in the evenings and at weekends, the rest of my friends disappeared from my life shortly after the funeral. Looking back, I guess they were far too young to truly understand, and I'm certain they weren't comfortable being with me, especially when I broke down. My adult friends and family, on the other hand, were able to give much more comfort and did not find it embarrassing if I cried.

Ultimately, it was about who I felt would listen and who I could talk to. Often, I would reflect on my dad at the most peculiar times, and so it was whoever just happened to be there that I would talk to. Those are the people I look back on as having been there for me; if more of my friends had been around at those moments, I feel we would have stayed close.

The people I was most drawn to were those who needed little warming up to the idea of talking about anything personal. Anyone who showed signs of self-consciousness around emotional conversations tended to make me clam up. I also found that people who were clearly too forced or who had an ulterior motive in getting me to open up made me feel awkward. A bit of compassion is usually all it takes for a comfortable conversation.

Compassion and a cat! My cat, Tom, was my rock. He would always find me when I was in a mess and would comfort me. He'd come and sit on me, put his paw on me and just look at me. I liked the idea that he could read me and just be there. Cats are an incredible force for me. I took comfort in my cat's concern for me. I didn't have to worry about his worry.

Friendships need to be two-way. I think people fear that if they are not acquainted with loss, they will be unable to support their friend, but what happens then is that a chasm forms between them. What they do not realise is that the best thing they can do is to offer small doses of normality – keeping up the routine of a friendship opens up a means to have fun and a forum to talk.

When I did eventually go back to school, everyone already knew what had happened, and it was nice not having to tell anyone. I'd done a lot of growing up by that time, so I felt more whole as a person – I felt prepared. People would come up and ask, 'Are you OK, man?' which was fine – what else could a kid ask? And I wanted people to acknowledge it – I'd have found it harder if they had ignored it. Generally, I look back on it as a happy return – no more lunchtimes crying in the toilets!

And Lastly ...

You don't need to be an expert in bereavement to be there for someone who has lost a loved one. Instead, you can be an expert in normality. My cousin was a perfect example of this. He'd come over most nights and would relay typical teenage stories, and tell me what others were doing. Sometimes he'd check in and ask if I was OK, then he'd slip back into a different role and talk video games. He treated me normally and didn't try to play the good listener all the time. It gets a bit boring after a while and sometimes you just need to forget.

What you can learn from Harry's story

There are two key themes here: being bereaved by suicide and being bereaved at a young age. If you know a bereaved young person, be mindful of the fact that most of their peers are not going to be equipped to support the person in the way they may need. Additionally, losing someone when you are young makes you grow up very fast, so the bereaved person will become even more isolated from their peer group. If you are young and reading this, don't be afraid of your friend; stick with them and remember they will still want to feel they have access to their friendship network. If you are an adult, stick with them even more, but remind them they are still young, and allowed to be so.

Feelings of blame and disapproval seem to be rife in the aftermath of suicide. While blame is not particularly useful for anyone, it is likely to be inevitable in these sorts of circumstances. Allow space for it, especially if the person is young. It may be the first emotion the person feels able to express, so don't block it, just make sure they don't become intoxicated by it.

Secondly, filter your own disapproval or feelings of disappointment, even if it's on behalf of the bereaved person. A child feels unconditional loyalty to their parents no matter how old they are, and if you try to challenge that or suggest they shouldn't, you are only going to create a wedge between you and them.

Chapter 13

Joy, whose husband died

I lost my husband, Alex, to cancer when I was fifty-five. We had been married for thirty-five years and 11 months. He was a strong, sociable and capable man with whom I had grown up. I admired him greatly and I still miss him six years on. I am glad we both knew what was about to happen, although there were only one or two days during the 'knowing' six months when we were really able to talk about it. On those days, he would just come out with something like, 'I'll be dead soon', and we would discuss what it was like knowing it was coming, and try to lovingly comfort each other. These were moments of openness between us, an acknowledgement. But most of the time it was our habit to be positive and to think that we would have longer than realistically was the case.

We would also work through the various concerns he had about leaving the family behind. He was worried that I didn't know how to run the house. We'd always had a fairly old-fashioned division of roles – he did the bills, I did the cooking – and so he worried he hadn't helped me enough to understand certain things. He also worried he hadn't seen everyone fulfil their potential, which in some ways he hadn't, like my promotion at work or meeting our grandchildren. But I tried to reassure him that he had seen the children through to a point where they were both grown up, happy and settled in life.

Unfortunately, neither of us knew it was going to be quite as soon as it was. Alex was still walking the day before he died. He'd been to hospital for some more radiation treatment for the pain and they wanted to keep him in overnight. He wanted to go home though. Marie, our daughter, came back from Edinburgh especially to see him, and he thought that was premature and that there'd be time to say goodbye later. She was fabulous, spending time with him by his bed. She brought him a banana and was so happy when he ate a tiny piece off the end to please her.

By the end of the day, I felt a little worried that Alex hadn't peed much – a sign that things weren't functioning well. But he just seemed so cheerful and sweet that I forgot about it.

We had recently moved him downstairs to a hospital bed in the sitting room and I was sleeping next to him on the sofa. At around 10 p.m., when we normally turned the light off to go to sleep, he became slightly irritable and told me to leave the light on. To my horror, looking back, I was rather cross and said I wouldn't be able to sleep with the light on. I can't imagine why I was so stubborn. About an hour after we'd gone to bed Alex became very angry and started to shout. He threw the covers back and tried to get out of bed, but fell on the floor. I asked if he needed the loo and he said no, he didn't know what he wanted. Marie came downstairs to help me get him back into bed, but he was hitting out and neither of us could move him. I've since learned that this is called 'terminal agitation' – literally fighting death, but at the time I didn't know this, and because it was such a physical problem and we couldn't get him comfortable again, I had to ring for an ambulance. My hope was that the paramedics would just put Alex back in bed, but they said they couldn't leave him there as he might hurt us or himself. Ambulances usually only take people to the nearest Accident & Emergency department, but this was absolutely not an option as far as I was concerned. So I called the hospital where Alex was a patient and begged them to take him without a scheduled admission. Eventually, they relented.

The journey to the hospital was horrific. Alex was strait-jacketed and utterly beside himself. Once we arrived I was terrified the doctors would give him something which would hasten his death. They promised they wouldn't, but explained that they had to give him something. Whatever it was, it calmed him immediately. I don't think he ever spoke to me again after that. He was assessed through the night and at 6 a.m. they told me he was dying and that he wouldn't be able to go home. Marie was at the hospital by this point, and we told my son, Chris, who was in Switzerland to come as quickly as possible. I kept talking to Alex, telling him how much I loved him and reminiscing over all the wonderful things we'd done together. I told him Chris was on his way, and we waited and waited. Tragically, Chris walked through the door just as they pronounced Alex dead. It was horrendous.

I hope and pray his final day was without distress, but I would never say his death was peaceful. I'm really sad it wasn't a better death.

What Does It Feel Like?

It was so awful that our darling Chris didn't make it. But we had a wonderful holiday together in France, during which Alex and Chris had spent some lovely evenings together, just the two of them, talking on the balcony, and Alex told me he felt they had said everything then that needed to be said. But of course, neither of them knew that would be the last time they'd see each other.

I wasn't aware of wanting anything in those first moments after Alex died. I didn't have a desperate need for anything in particular. I felt pretty empty and numb, but I guess I was in shock. We all were. I can't remember how I got home, but I just know we were all incredibly sad together.

I expected to cope and so I did. I have a profession to which I knew I could return in due course and two successful and delightful children of whom I am very proud. I did find I was affected very much by sadness and loneliness in other people though and found myself weeping when a very small old lady bought herself a single bun in the bakery. I don't think this was about my own loneliness – I never felt afraid of being alone – I just had a greatly heightened sense of suffering and perception of the sadness of life for many people.

I consider myself to be less sociable and generally less fun now than I was when Alex was alive, and I think that's also how I felt in the first few months. I knew I would miss the person I was, that I had been with my husband, and to this day, I still do. I can't get her back. I just feel less interesting now than I did then. I was married from the age of eighteen to fifty-five. For so many years I had this identity as the wife of a nice-looking and clever husband and mother to two lovely children. That was my point of reference – it was who I was. Now that's gone, so within about five minutes of meeting people, I find myself longing to tell them: ' I was married you know, for thirty-five years, and he was like this and we did that ... ' Obviously, I try not to say it though. I assume most people won't want to know. And, in any case, as you get older, you make fewer new friends, really.

Having said that, I have made two new friends and they are

especially important to me, since I also lost my best friend two years ago. I got to know them while dog-walking and I'm really glad to have them, but I don't need anyone else.

What Can You Say – and Avoid Saying?

I was really bad at telling people. I phoned the most significant people and my best friend put a notice in the newspaper. But there were lots of people I did not tell. I'm not sure why I didn't because there were so many people who I really liked and wanted to have around, but who had no idea what had happened and so didn't attend the funeral. Then I found myself feeling upset and thinking, Where are they?

I also told only one colleague at work and asked him not to tell others by email. Yet, strangely, I would tell strangers at the drop of a hat. In fact, I did tell almost anyone who crossed my path. So perhaps I was just anti-email; or maybe it was something about being in control of the delivery of the news. I didn't like the idea of people talking about Alex's death without me, or it being gossip. Maybe that's a way of seeking sympathy, I don't know. But as much as I couldn't bear giving someone else the job of passing on the news on the one hand, I couldn't face ringing round everyone myself either. I wasn't exactly maximising my chances of getting loving support!

The most comforting words from people were those about Alex. For me, a person is not dead as long as there are still people living who can remember them. So anyone who remembered Alex with love and fondness and expressed empathy with his suffering was a comfort to me. But those people who were feeling for me rather than considering him annoyed me. I wanted them to be sad he was dead and to miss him like I did; and I wanted them to do this without me prompting them. I remember thinking at times, Why aren't they saying more about Alex? I am well aware of how harsh and ungrateful this sounds, but that was my honest reaction; I felt a strong need to protect Alex's memory and who he was. I knew that he'd sometimes put people's backs up, and so I worried that this is what they'd remember. But did everyone realise what a fantastic person he was? Did they all know the good things about him, of which there were so many? I would have appreciated more people being willing and able to talk about him as an individual. I often look around now and think, Who still remembers Alex?

I also liked people who were direct – those who would phone and be forthcoming with their support and thoughts. The hospice nurse paid us a visit and was rather matter of fact. I think she was trying to mirror my own manner. To be honest, what I liked most was if people were sad. I particularly liked seeing one couple who had been very close to Alex because they cried a lot for him with me. That was nice. I felt better for knowing that they missed him so much.

When it comes to letters, I personally try and say something like, 'I will always think of X doing this ... ' So inevitably, the letters that stood out for me were those that included recollections of Alex and his life. One of the best ones I received was written a good five years after his death. The person had not written at the time, but years later he obviously felt able to do so. The letter was a sort of analysis of Alex's character. It was critical in parts and, on the whole, it was a very balanced account. It was interesting and I treasure it because it painted a very clear picture of my husband in writing; it is better than a photograph.

One thing people always tell you after someone dies is that you shouldn't make hasty decisions. I'm inclined to think this isn't necessarily right though. I wanted to move house quite early on and I think that if I'd done so, it wouldn't have been a bad thing.

What Helped – and What Didn't?

I rang my best friend when I got home from the hospital and she came over the next day. She drove me around doing various errands, like collecting the death certificate, etc. I felt very comfortable with her and she came back again the next day to help start the funeral arrangements and get the documents for the solicitor ready. She also did things like help me choose what to wear for the funeral and take my clothes to the dry cleaners before the cremation service.

On the whole I didn't have that many people around me. But I think that was OK. I remember a distinct need for everything to be organised – the house, paperwork, cupboards – and I got very involved with all of that. Anyone who helped with that reorganisation was a godsend, but there weren't that many offers and, in retrospect, I think I'd have appreciated more. I don't know how I could have asked though. At my age, people are very busy with work, family, etc. So in the end I paid someone to come and help.

I suppose the sorting gave me a sense of control – over myself and the future. I live in a big house, and had never had to run it or be alone there; I wanted to feel able and not oppressed by too much stuff. Also, all Alex's stuff had got on my nerves for years and now I had my chance to clear things! It did make me feel better.

I had a helpful neighbour who came round with magazines for me and asked me for supper, but again, I often felt she didn't say enough nice things about Alex. She was kind and practical and asked how I was, but I desperately wanted Alex to be remembered.

Thankfully, I didn't notice embarrassment in others. I cried often, even in shops and on buses, especially if I saw someone who looked lonely. I think if anything, I was surprised at how easily others dealt with me.

We had two funerals for Alex. I'm not sure why. I think I wanted to get the cremation out of the way, but didn't think I could organise the service he wanted in time. The two occasions were very different. One was just a service at which Chris spoke. I was so proud of him. All the most important people to me were there – my mother, my best friend, my children – and I think it holds a more precious place in my memory.

The second service was harder than the first in a way because it was a bit later, and at that stage you're much more taken up with feeling the person's absence. But it had to be done and I did it. Because I hadn't notified everyone there were people missing, and I was sad they weren't there – they'd have enjoyed it very much, so I really rather regret that. Nevertheless, it was entirely bearable, mostly helped by the fact that Alex had been very precise about the music he wanted played (which a kind friend of my daughter downloaded and put on a CD) and he had written thoughts on each piece which my children read aloud. This gave a focus and structure to the whole thing. I don't have any regrets about having the second service, but it probably would have been just as good to have one occasion.

A couple of Alex's friends were particularly helpful in a practical way. Firstly, they kept in touch every month by writing to me, which was wonderful. And they helped me sell Alex's vintage Alpha Romeos and Dinky car collection. I've since lost touch with one of them, but that's just as much my fault as his.

How people can get through these things without family I

have no idea. My children and mother made me feel OK. My heart breaks seeing what the children are going through, but I was so grateful for them and proud of them.

I went back to work about five months after Alex died. By that time I hadn't worked for seven months as I had stopped when he needed daily care. I think I felt ready to go back and it was actually quite good. It was an environment I felt very happy in. Returning, as a widow, was surprisingly OK, as although I hadn't asked any of my colleagues to the funeral, they were all very kind. People seem prepared to forgive everything at these times and they were all very understanding. I don't think I had very much help or discussion from them, but I did feel that they were there and that I was recognised as someone who had just lost her husband, so I didn't feel pressured into getting better.

Having said that, I do still find it difficult six years on when people don't remember Alex, especially on the anniversary. But people have their own lives and I think there is a limit to what you can reasonably expect in terms of recognition and support. Nevertheless, I can't deny my feelings and it is a lovely thing if someone does acknowledge it ... I really like it.

So for me, the person who makes their presence really felt is the one who continues to remember the deceased and who is unafraid to talk about them.

And Lastly ...

Don't constantly tell the person how you felt when you were bereaved or how it affected you, but rather always keep the deceased and who they are in mind. Death is a part of life and it must be accepted and incorporated into the lives of those who remain.

What you can learn from Joy's story

Joy talks of how her identity was largely dependent on her relationship with her husband. That means that when he died, she not only lost him, but she also lost the part of herself she most confidently identified with. It was, in effect, a double loss and so she not only had to adapt to life without him, but had to reconfigure who she is without her husband. Help your friends tune in with their true self, the part that exists with or without partners. Help them discover who they really are and encourage them to trust they have all the tools within themselves to be the person they want to be.

Joy also interestingly liked it when people shared her loss. This contrasts to some other contributors, so again, use your wisdom and take clues from how they respond to you. If they seem comforted when you express your own pain, then express it more. If they become withdrawn and shut down, then put the focus back on them.

Chapter 14

Norman, whose brother died

My brother, Tony, died two years ago, unexpectedly, at the age of sixty-three. He had been ill on and off for a number of years with an autoimmune disease and hadn't thought he'd make it to sixty, but it still came as a real shock. It was so sudden. He was flying home to Canada, fell asleep on the plane and never woke up. He was dead when the plane landed. His wife rang me in tears a few hours later. I didn't know how to react. I think my first thought was, Poor wife and kids; what can I do to help them? She asked if I would tell my mum and sister, Sally.

I had been picking apples when the phone rang and I wanted to finish the task before doing anything else. I think I felt this mundane activity would allow me to think through what I would do next. My wife offered to come with me to London to tell my sister, who had been incredibly close to Tony, and my ninety-eight-year-old mum, but I told her not to as she had something important to do that I didn't want her to miss.

I ended up having to tell Sally on the phone, as she was teaching. She was hysterical. We then told our mum together, who was amazingly stoical about it. I'd thought it would kill her, but she didn't even cry. She'd been as aware as we all were that Tony might have died, but maybe because she'd been through such dreadful things in her life, her previous experiences of grief had prepared her – I don't know. Still, telling her was a really tough moment. After that Sally and I desperately wanted a drink: all we had was rum, which neither of us likes, but we drank it anyway. Then Sally went home to prepare to go to Canada for the funeral. I wasn't going to attend, as someone needed to look after Mum. I stayed by her bedside, but after a while she told me she was OK and that I should go home. It was rather a relief, actually. There was only so much we could say in those circumstances – I can't think of anything worse than losing your child. If one of my children died I'd be inconsolable.

What Does It Feel Like?

It's always a shock, even when you think you're prepared. When they actually die, it's so final. My mother is now over 100 and a half. There's no doubt she is going to die soon, but I know it will still be a shock when it happens. And I have no idea how to prepare for it.

My brother and I weren't very close. He lived in Canada and had a successful career as a doctor and celebrity. In fact, he'd once saved my life in his capacity as an oncologist by insisting that I had a colonoscopy even when my GP had found nothing wrong with me. The test revealed cancer of the colon which was successfully dealt with. Nevertheless, I wasn't much moved by his absence.

Tony was my baby brother – younger than me by seven years – and part of that dynamic, I guess, is that he was intensely annoying. He had difficult relationships with his children and both his wives and although I felt sorry for him, it also irritated me that he didn't do something about it. I feel I should miss him more. But I don't. I loved him, but I didn't like him very much. You don't have to like your family.

Sally adored him though, so she was incredibly sad at his loss. I didn't find it strange that we didn't share this emotion. I was comforted by the fact that I had to be the responsible adult; I liked being in the role of the consoler, rather than the consoled. I wanted to be there for her. You conquer your fears when you are forced to face them – like when you hear a noise in the house when your children are asleep and you know you have to act confidently and bravely. Similarly, I knew automatically what my role had to be, and I was OK about it. And I think Tony would have approved too.

I don't think bereavement is necessarily about weeping. I never wept for my friend who died when he was twenty-four. And even after losing my father I only wept when I saw a film that reminded me of him. I guess that kind of expression of grief is just not for me; which is surprising really, as I do cry very easily, especially since I've had children. But everyone misses people in different ways, and it's easy to feel guilt if you don't express grief in the way people expect you to.

What Can You Say – and Avoid Saying?

I got over the shock of Tony's death by telling others about it. In a way, when you mention the death of someone close, especially to people who didn't know them, there's an odd satisfaction in seeing their reaction because it's an interruption of normal social dynamics. And that's sort of what you want after someone has died – for a bit, anyway. I know that sounds a bit selfish, but I think one can be quite selfish in grief. And because I felt guilty at not feeling more emotion, perhaps other people's expression of sympathy made me feel better about what was lacking in my own experience of grief.

There's something about the death of a celebrity that has a wider resonance. This meant that we received a lot of letters from

Tony's professional colleagues, who wrote funny anecdotes about his public life. It seemed that that was what most people picked up on, rather than the intimate details of his behind-the-scenes character. I would have preferred letters talking about Tony's personal life, but I didn't get them. I've always prided myself on being honest about what I'm feeling in condolence letters without being hurtful. I think if you're honest, then you'll be fine.

At the memorial we organised for Tony in London six months later, one woman told my mother that Tony had proposed to her twice. I thought it was quite funny, but everyone else was outraged, especially Tony's widow. I think the problem was that she was expressing her own grief and was being too self-absorbed with the wrong person and at the wrong time. Even though she hadn't intended to be funny, I found it amusing, and I think Tony would have too – Tony was like a professional comedian, so it seemed right for something humorous to happen at his memorial.

The wisest words I heard were from my wife. We had talked before about preparing for loss and death, and she always said that actually the grown-up thing is to not try and prepare. All we can do is wait and see what it's like when it actually happens. Then we just have to try and pick ourselves up.

What Helped – and What Didn't?

There weren't that many practicalities for us to deal with after Tony died because, of course, everything was dealt with over in Canada. That meant there wasn't an enormous amount for people to help out with. I didn't find it hard not going to the funeral. In a way I was slightly relieved, as I didn't get on that well with Tony's wife. If I'd been there I'd have got in the way. It also felt important to be with Mum, who couldn't go.

For the memorial in London – to which Mum went, two days before her ninety-ninth birthday – we asked people to contribute to a charity in Tony's memory. Asking for money is always tricky. I regarded this as a charity, but it was still incredibly hard to raise money. We were surprised by those who did contribute, but even more by those who didn't, and we only just limped to our target for the first year. I thought we'd raise a lot more. All those hundreds of people had expressed their love and yet there was little follow-through.

We did have some great support in other respects though. One of Tony's friends flew over to give an address at his funeral in Canada, and also took charge of the memorial in London. He wasn't the easiest person to work with, but Tony would have been pleased with the result. He spoke beautifully, and got very involved. We were enormously grateful for this help and support and his very apparent dedication to honouring Tony's memory.

It was a surprise to read all the tributes from people and hear how Tony had touched and changed their lives. As his older brother, I'd had little idea about how much he would be missed by those outside his family. And only now am I realising the impact that these tributes have made on my experience of grief, as they have highlighted just how much I undervalued him.

I'm sorry I undervalued him. I'm only now articulating some-thing I couldn't before. I don't think he ever needed my approval, but you always want to be valued by the people you respect and admire and love. So I feel a bit bad about not giving that approval. He could be such a presumptuous little bugger though, and the desire to put him down was sometimes too tempting. But I can see now I could have been kinder. Perhaps I was withholding admiration, which I might have been wiser to give. I wish I'd been more generous.

Where words may fail at funerals and memorials, I am a great endorser of hugs. Or the handshake and soulful look is also fine. I sometimes think a hug tells you all you need to know, especially, say, from a relative you haven't seen for twenty years – what else can you do? You don't want to 'catch up' with them, and you might not even like them very much, so a hug can be useful. Not everyone can be ready with an original statement, and sometimes people are genuinely at a loss for words because of sadness and shock, and that should be honoured. So the instinctive action is the best. Don't be ashamed of it. I got lots of hugs from my wife and children and sister and that was just the ticket. I know they meant it.

My two daughters were much more concerned about me than I was about myself. They thought I'd be more upset than I was, but were loving enough not to probe, and just to be there for me. I wasn't being brave or detached. I was just being how I felt. I wasn't trying to manufacture grief.

One of them took time off work to come and stay with me while my wife was away on business because she didn't want me to be alone. I told her I'd be fine, but I was glad she came. We spent a wonderful time together, chatting, drinking and reminiscing. It was lovely.

People need to know what to expect from you at a funeral, especially if, for example, you're giving a tribute. I always tell the bereaved family what I'm going to say first, so they know. But when it's one-to-one, I prefer going from the heart. When you have just lost someone close, then you just want to be around honesty. So if you feel you can't say anything, it's best not to. A soulful squeeze is better than empty words.

I think to be there means being able to talk openly about the good and bad things you remember, and to laugh and cry. I got strength and energy from my immediate family. Every death leaves a hole with jagged edges. The hole may grow smaller in time, but you're always going to snag your emotions on those edges – they never smooth over. Each 'hole' is very individual, and there is no one rule that works for everyone, but I would say, trust your instincts, rather than your intellect, and say what you feel about the dead person to the bereaved.

And Lastly ...

Talk about it and don't feel guilty. The more honest you are, the more it will be appreciated. Be instinctive and don't prepare a speech. I always send the first draft of a condolence letter – because the more you practise, the more artificial it becomes.

What you can learn from Norman's story

Norman tells us he wasn't terribly moved by his brother's death. But not being affected, while others around you are, might be rather isolating so don't lessen your support just because you believe that to be the case with your friend. They are still entitled to a bit of extra TLC.

It wasn't until I interviewed Norman that he tapped in to his feelings of guilt about not valuing his brother. That was several years after his death. Just as you strive to accept your bereaved friend's way of coping, don't take everything at face value – be open to the possibility that there may be more there to be uncovered. That doesn't mean you have to prod and probe, but simply bear it in mind that some things take a long time to surface.

Chapter 15

Lina, whose friend died

My friend Gemma died aged 24. She was diagnosed with cancer nine months before, and throughout that time I had been supporting her through her chemotherapy and radiotherapy treatment. During this time I developed an eating disorder, and am still in recovery, so her death has been very much tied up with my own illness and recovery, making it difficult for me to grieve solely for her and to separate it from what is happening to me.

Gemma is the first friend I remember having as a child, and she was my only friend for a long time when we were young. We met at infant school and as soon as we were old enough, we walked to school together every day until the end of secondary school. From then on, we started to change and differed in terms of what we were into, what we did at weekends and who we hung out with. But we maintained a bond throughout that went beyond distance and phases.

All through Gemma's illness, I was never aware of any kind of prognosis. She didn't talk about whether she was dying and we focused very much on how the treatment was going. We would often talk about what she was going to do when she got better.

This meant I was never quite sure if and when the 'dying' conversation would happen. I kept expecting us to have deep and meaningful discussions about life and death, but we would just chat about everyday things. I would sometimes wake up in the night with a start when I was staying with her and ask, 'Is there anything you want to say? Are you OK?' but she would just laugh and say, 'I'm fine, Lina. Go back to sleep.'

I remember thinking at one point that things seemed to be deteriorating, and asked her dad, 'Is this when I should take more time off work to see Gemma and tell other friends to come and see her too?' He just said, 'I don't think we're at that stage just yet.' So as long as nobody else was saying Gemma was going to die, I felt I couldn't possibly think it or say it either.

Then, two weeks before she died, I was diagnosed with anorexia. I'd gone to see a family friend who was a psychiatrist and told him about Gemma. He said, 'Supporting a dying friend is very difficult', and I told him he'd got it wrong – that Gemma wasn't dying. So he told me very frankly that once the cancer is in your liver and bones it's not going away. But I kept resisting the information and he went on reasserting it until eventually he said: 'You already know this Lina … look at what you're doing to yourself.' And that's basically how I found out Gemma was dying. Everything suddenly made sense. It was like a light being switched on. I remember speaking to my boyfriend afterwards and feeling really calm. I didn't have to pretend any more, or be strong or confused about why I was so upset. It was OK for me to be ill and sad about things.

I sensed that things were getting worse and then one day, two weeks later, I found myself spending a lot of time looking at my phone, waiting for a text from Gemma's family to tell me to come and say my last goodbye. Instead, I got a phone call from her sister telling me she'd died.

I felt a lightness in the air as soon as I heard the words. I felt Gemma's soul had been released from her suffering body and that she was now everywhere. Now that she had died we were able to face the thing we'd been hiding from for so long. Her sister asked me to pass on the news of her death, which I agreed to do instinctively. I remember telling one friend who was shocked and devastated, and found myself thinking, 'Well, what did you expect? You obviously haven't been around that much.' I can now see how quickly I had changed from being the unknowing, hopeful friend like this girl to the one who was prepared.

What Does It Feel Like?

None of it was like I had imagined it would be. I had quite a Hollywood view of death and grief and thought I'd collapse on the floor and cry for help. But when Gemma's sister told me I thought: Oh shit, we didn't get to do our big last-goodbye. There was no hysteria, just a calm acceptance that she was dead, that the thing we'd all been thinking and not saying had now happened. I remember the sky was really lovely that day, and I thought the sun was shining even more because she'd died. I didn't expect to have that kind of spiritual experience.

I also thought the actual dying process itself would have been more like it is in the films – that we'd know Gemma was dying and how long she had left to live. I thought she would lose her hair and we would spend time choosing headscarves and hats to wear. I thought she'd be breaking down and telling me how scared she was about dying. I thought there would be life-affirming conversations and that we'd spend time making memory books and saying all the things we'd never get to say again.

Following the family's lead all the time had been quite exhausting – preparing and preparing for the conversation that never happened, trying to be upbeat and entertaining, but also always open and ready in case anyone did want to talk 'death'. It was like being on high alert, being really vigilant all the time. It made it hard for me. I feel bad saying that, because it obviously wasn't as bad for me as it was for Gemma, but it was difficult. All this and the fact that I wasn't family or even in the same city had made it challenging to reach out and ask for support.

It was only afterwards that I learned they had all had an awareness Gemma was dying, including Gemma herself. I found out that she'd known when I saw a documentary she'd participated in about what it was like to be dying. There's a part where she explains why she doesn't feel angry about dying at such a young age. She says quite calmly, 'Well, this is my path'. It was such a shock to see that – to see her so at ease with the fact that she was dying – but it was also a bit of a relief to know that she'd gone through all that with such awareness. My dad described her as the Buddha enlightened, really accepting of her path and mindful of what was going on.

The complicated thing with seeing a friend die is that you're always aware that whatever pain or sadness you're feeling isn't as bad as what the family are going through. I didn't allow myself to do anything pleasurable (e.g. relax, go out, have sex, eat nice food) because I didn't want to be 'having fun' while Gemma was going through such a difficult, pleasure-less, painful time. I was denying myself life.

Sadly, things changed with Gemma's parents after she died.

While Gemma was ill I was really welcomed by them – it reminded me of when we were younger – and I felt a strong connection with them. They were always happy to see me and I got a lot of positive reinforcement from them every time I visited Gemma. Her mum taught me to knit and she reassured me that I was allowed to have problems because of Gemma's illness.

The day she died, everything changed. I went to the hospice with a few other friends and her parents seemed uncomfortable having us there. Even though I am aware it may be because it was too painful for them to see me there still alive, I was shocked and hurt and hadn't expected it to be that way. We've had a handful of nice times since then – on Gemma's birthday, for example – but mostly I have felt quite uncomfortable. I've now come to accept that I won't have the relationship with her parents I had hoped for, but I have maintained a natural, close relationship with Gemma's sister, which means a lot to me.

In fact, Gemma's sister now has a friend who has cancer. I was talking to her about it recently and she told me how she wants to stop working so she can spend time with her friend, and how difficult it is when you're not part of the immediate family because you don't know the role you're meant to play. She looked at me then in recognition of how hard it had been for me. I accepted her acknowledgement – it was brilliant and I feel something really changed in that moment.

What Can You Say – and Avoid Saying?

I called my parents as soon as I found out and my dad asked what I wanted. I said I didn't know – I didn't know what was allowed or whether any help was justified. He then told me that now was the time for me to ask them for help. And so I asked him to come and pick me up from Manchester. It was great being given permission to ask for help.

As long as it came from an authentic place anyone who provided good feedback about me or gave me something to feel OK about was greatly appreciated. My boss used to remind me that Gemma's illness would be having a big impact on my own well-being, which was always reassuring and supportive.

It was also hugely reassuring when people said, 'You did enough' – to know there was nothing else I could have done. I doubted these things all the time – wondering if I should have gone to see Gemma more, if I was a good enough friend. I was fortunate that many of my friends took the time to comfort me, and texted me saying things like, 'Gemma is now free, so you can be too', 'It must be hard for you, I know how close you were to Gemma' or, 'You have been such a good friend to Gemma.'

When my eating disorder was becoming more apparent, towards the end of Gemma's illness, my mum said, 'You not eating isn't going to save Gemma', and that was also wonderful to hear.

Two weeks before Gemma died I saw a crystal energy healer. At the end of the session she said, 'Hopefully I've made you able to experience what's going on. Being with a friend who is dying is one of the most beautiful experiences we have.' This was really nice to hear, especially as a psychiatrist had told me not to see Gemma any more. I was grateful for the healer's confidence in me to be strong enough to be a supportive friend to Gemma.

What didn't work was when people said things like, 'Gemma wouldn't want this'. When people tried to speak from Gemma's perspective, I felt protective and defensive. Of course

I knew Gemma wouldn't want me to cope in such a self-destructive way and I felt completely ashamed that I had reacted like that, but I couldn't just turn it off and it wasn't helpful to hear. The people around me supporting me were my friends, not Gemma's and so I wanted them to praise what I was doing, rather than predict what my friend might think and feel. Even positive assumptions like 'Gemma loved you' were annoying.

I remember a lot of people getting frustrated that I was still grieving and not letting myself indulge in life's pleasures. A few months ago I was talking to someone about Gemma's death and they said, 'You're over that now though, aren't you?' I tried to explain that it doesn't work like that, but I'm not sure how much it registered.

Someone else responded to me telling them about my experience by saying, 'Whoa! That's deep', or something to that effect. I had thought we could share that kind of intimate stuff, but her comment made me realise I'd got it wrong, which made me feel pretty uncomfortable.

People's approach to me changed noticeably after Gemma died – it had to. Before she died, all their questions were about her – how she was, how the treatment was going, when I was next seeing her; afterwards, they were all about me. I think that's because people find it easier to ask about cancer and the practical issues around it than to delve into the deeper questions about what it's like to see a friend dying. And from my perspective as well, it was easier to keep the focus on Gemma, rather than my own emotions about it all. But grief isn't an illness, and because it was no longer possible for people to hide behind those practical questions once Gemma had died, the emphasis shifted to me. I'm grateful that my friends and family were able to make that shift. It felt very natural.

What Helped – and What Didn't?

I got a lot of support from work in particular. My boss encouraged me to talk to my parents, speak to a doctor and have time off and counselling through a scheme at work. She was always making sure I was OK, in contrast to friends and family who were often (understandably) asking after Gemma's family.

I became aware of a sort of 'competitive grief' that other friends of Gemma noticed too. I would be resentful if old school friends came to me crying about Gemma's death, if they hadn't been around during her illness. I would feel angry that they had no idea how her family, flatmate and close friends had been feeling all this time. A mutual friend mentioned it at the funeral and was very open with her anger towards all these people who hadn't seen Gemma for ages and were now crying so much. Gemma's sister just said, 'They're all sad because Gemma's dead and that's all that matters'. Although it sounds awful to say this, I thought that because she was Gemma's sister she didn't have anything to prove – her closeness to Gemma was a given, whereas for me it did feel important to be recognised, and for the specialness of our friendship to be acknowledged.

I wanted to be around my parents a lot, and I needed to cry all the time. I rejected a lot of love and support from friends, other family members and my boyfriend because I didn't feel I deserved it. My way of asking for support was by having a breakdown and not being able to do anything at all. Things had to reach crisis point for me to accept support. I remember lots of emergency trips home, being fed, put to bed and stroked. I couldn't just say 'give me a hug' if it wasn't crisis point.

Even though my close relatives were grieving for Gemma as well, I felt I was allowed to be the main grieving person with them, whereas with Gemma's family, understandably, I was not. This was also true of my friends who didn't know Gemma and it felt important to have access to this kind of grieving space. They were incredibly supportive and sat with me all evening the day Gemma died, until my dad and sister had arrived to collect me. They must have had other things to do or places to be, but they were there for me and that felt incredibly comforting.

Gemma's funeral was the day before my birthday so as a birthday gift, my boyfriend (now fiancé) took me away the day after. This was a much needed chance for us to 'regroup' and make up for the time we had lost. It was just what I needed.

I didn't help organise the funeral or wake, but I was charged with informing Gemma's friends about the details. I found this less difficult than telling people she'd died as I did it all via email or text, so didn't have to deal with their reactions.

Quite often I was aware of people wanting to change the subject when I spoke about Gemma, and I'd think, How can we talk about anything else when something so awful has happened? I don't think I ever said it to anyone though. For me, Gemma was all I could think and talk about at the time, and I found it difficult to concentrate on anything else.

I cried a lot and, on the whole, people were very supportive if I broke down. I remember breaking down in restaurants and going to the loo because I didn't feel it was appropriate to cry in such a public place. Sometimes, if I knew I was going to cry, I'd pre-empt it and tell people, 'Look, I'm OK crying, do you mind if I go ahead?'

Crying is good, and it needs to happen. I was once with my boyfriend at a music festival after Gemma had died and I just cried through a whole set. I stood there, crying, listening to the music, looking at the stars. It felt like my whole body was grieving and it was such a release. Dave was behind me and he held me up, so I could just let it happen.

When I speak to people now who didn't know Gemma and I see them cry, it's really nice. I know they're crying for me as well as for what happened, and it feels very different from the people who were bawling their eyes out at the funeral just because of their own pain and loss.

I think my relationships changed a lot with some people, but I feel they were all made stronger in some way. Being there is about allowing the person to grieve freely in the way they want and need to, unless this is causing them harm, in which case encouraging them to express their feelings in a guilt-free way with compassion in your heart is the best thing you can do – giving them time, love and a safe space in which to express themselves and listening without judgement and with acceptance.

And Lastly . . .

Look after yourself! Even if you're not the one who has lost someone, supporting the person who has can be hard and brings up difficult emotions which shouldn't be overlooked.

It's also important to remember that the person shouldn't feel rushed or pressured to feel any different. They shouldn't compare themselves to other people who are also grieving, believing, for example, that they shouldn't be so sad because they are not the mum/sister/partner of the person who died. If you're sad, you're sad because it's had an effect on you for whatever reason and that is OK. So as a friend to the bereaved friend, it's really helpful to remind them of this.

What you can learn from Lina's story

Often, after a lengthy dying process, the first thing the
bereaved feel is relief. This might be truer with people in
Lina's position, when her role in the support dynamic was
rather complex and she was carrying a lot of uncertainty. Don't
be afraid to share the relief with your friend or loved one.

They may also need rather a lot of reassuring, like Lina, that it
is OK to ask for help. Remind them that you are there for
them, not the bereaved family, and that they are allowed to find
the process painful.

Finally, I think this story brings to the fore the role of the best
friend. We label some friends 'best' for a reason – they are in
some way special, more precious to us perhaps, and so it is
important for this relationship to be acknowledged when
someone loses their best friend. I know it might sound a bit
inane in light of the circumstances, but these seemingly
unimportant distinctions can be enormously reassuring and
help them express their grief more freely.

Chapter 16

Ben, whose partner died

Lizzie and I met when I was 25 and had been together for a year and a half. Some wouldn't consider that a very long time, but I'd been on my own for three years when we found each other out of millions of people in the world. She was my partner. She was my best friend.

I was at work, and at the end of the day I went to check my phone. I'd sent Lizzie a text in the morning saying, 'Have a good day', and I hadn't heard back from her, which was unusual. Instead I had a voicemail from her sister. That was unusual too. I listened to the message telling me she had bad news and saying I should call as soon as possible. I knew straight away that Lizzie was dead. I could hear it in her sister's voice. I immediately rang back, hoping against hope, telling myself it could be something else. I rang and said, 'Tell me, tell me right now', and she just said, 'I'm so sorry, Ben'. I kept begging her to tell me it wasn't true, to tell me it was a sick joke: 'Please tell me it's a joke ... please, please.' Then I put the phone down and I just howled. It was animalistic.

Lizzie had been killed in a cycling accident on her way to work. When I sent her my text message, she'd been dead for thirty-three minutes.

I phoned my best friend straight away and told him to come and get me. Then I phoned my mum and said: 'She's dead.' Mum asked, 'Who is?' I told her it was Lizzie and that I had to go and I'd call her back. Then I went to try and find the office manager. I remember tearing around the building, down the stairs, trying to find him, shouting out his name. I finally ran into a room where I found another colleague. I screamed out, 'Oh my God, she's dead', and I just fell into his arms. After that I spent a lot of time on the phone, telling people. Then I went through some work handover bits and pieces, and before I left the manager told me to take two weeks off. But at that point I had no idea what I wanted.

That evening I smoked a lot of weed in an attempt to persuade my mind into believing something else. I managed to convince myself that I had lost it, that I had had a psychotic episode and that I was waiting to be taken away to an institution. The next day I texted my friend saying, 'Tell me it didn't happen', and he just replied saying, 'I'm so sorry man'.

Three days later I went to see Lizzie's body in the hospital. Her family told me they were going and I knew I had to go too. I don't know why, but I did. There was no doubt in my mind. I was so frightened. I was walking to a hospital to look at a dead person. That's scary enough. But add to that what that person means to you and it's horrific.

Her family went in first and I waited. I won't forget the moment Lizzie's mum came out. She just said my name, over and over again, crying. I hugged her and then went into the room. She still looked like her. She'd died from a heart attack, so her face only had a couple of scratches. I didn't cry. I just spoke to her. Part of me thought she was still alive – I kept wanting her to wake up, but I was also always conscious that I was talking to the person I love on a mortuary slab in a hospital. I left the room shaking uncontrollably. It's awful reliving it now. Those images don't go; they will never leave me.

I went to see Lizzie three times at the chapel of rest too. She was in a dress that I recognised, which had been altered to make it shorter, wearing a brooch I knew a story about and tights that she'd worn when I first met her. And she wasn't alive. She was still beautiful. She was just very, very cold. I was kissing the forehead of someone in a coffin who, just a few nights before, I had kissed goodnight.

I didn't cry. I felt I needed to be brave for her. But I broke down as soon as I walked out. Then her father gestured for me to go back in again after he and Lizzie's mum had been in. I later found out this was because her mum was worried that if Lizzie could still see anything, she didn't want her last image to be of her parents distraught at her side; she wanted it to be me saying, 'It'll be all right. I'll see you soon.' Now I also have in my mind that I was the last person to ever see her.

What Does It Feel Like?

I don't think the word 'never' is ever truly relevant unless you're talking about death. I will *never* see this person again. I can *never* change anything about that. That's it. It's really final. The only thing that is certain is that death is certain. 'Never' has been an important word to me. I still don't understand it – maybe I will in time, I don't know.

I've never felt so alone. I have very good friends and an amazing family and they all help me as much as they can. But I still feel alone, even though I have all these people around me. Lizzie was my best friend. She was my family. She was my partner. And in a situation like this she'd be the first person I'd want to speak to.

I feel pointless, lost, guilty. I feel like I am losing my sanity. I have seen things that will change my world for ever, that literally have blown my mind. I know I could put myself in a darkened room and not come out. But I also know I have to get on with things, carry on with life. And I know I would be halting a process – the process of grief. Lizzie would not want me to do that.

I know I need help, though in what form has yet to be discovered. I think I needed – and need – someone to say it's not real. Impossible, I know, but I still seek this desperately.

For the first few weeks, I felt comfortable asking for help – able to ring people and talk about it, ask for their time. I don't do that so much now. Life has to go on for others and you can't expect people to be there all the time. I feel now that I don't want to disturb or tell people how I'm really feeling. I have learned to live with my own company.

I ask my mum and a very specific set of friends for help. My needs vary: sometimes I need to be around people, and other times I don't want to speak to anyone; sometimes I just shut down – I feel that what everyone else is talking about is trivial and I just can't enter into the conversation. It is difficult because I don't know what I'm going to want or when; so suddenly, I might need to see someone I haven't spoken to for a while and that might be quite unsettling for people around me, but that's how it happens – it just arrives out of the blue.

It's very difficult not being part of the family of the person who died. Even if we'd been engaged or married, we're still not blood-tied, so it's very different. The way I see it is quite simply, that I can't talk to them about how I feel. It's a different pain. I know I feel a different grief to Lizzie's mum.

I haven't seen a bereavement specialist yet. I have, however, seen my psychiatrist. I have been with him for several years for different reasons. He is honest and blunt, bordering on rude, but I like that very much. I found it difficult that he said I should think about putting my photos of Lizzie away in a memory box in a few months. He also thought I should start to try and dissociate myself from the family. Based on his previous knowledge of me, he was concerned that the photos and memories could lead me to a dangerous place. I think he's right, especially about my relationship with the family. In five years, I might have moved on, I might have another partner; but Lizzie's mother will never have a daughter again. But it's horrific to think about all that right now. And I can't get rid of anything yet. I have a bear she bought me and a photo and a necklace that go everywhere with me. Wherever I sleep I put the photo up, and my screensaver is a painting that someone did of her. Maybe, in time, I'll have to put these things away, but right now, I need to keep her alive.

I went back to work two days after the funeral. I'd had my two weeks off and was worried that if I didn't go back they'd replace me and then what would I do? If I'd given up my job what would Lizzie have thought? I spent a lot of time thinking about what she would want. It was difficult though. I didn't know my colleagues, so I spent a lot of time crying in a room alone, then reappearing as though everything was OK.

What Can You Say – and Avoid Saying?

After I had been to see Lizzie's body, I met up with a friend. He asked me if when I saw her, I felt a difference between body and soul. My response was that her body was there in front of me, but that her soul was in us – the people who went into the room. I was grateful for the chance to explore the experience in that way: it was quite an unusual question to ask, and I hadn't thought about it like that, but in considering it, I was brought to the idea that Lizzie was still alive in some way, in me. So his curiosity helped me to think more clearly.

I found it most comforting when people said things like, 'Contact me any time of day or night', or, 'Be, just be', as this assured me that anything I was feeling was OK. One new friend told me straight away that this would be the worst thing that would ever happen to me. True or not, the honesty and bluntness felt right – they didn't try to tiptoe around what had happened or diminish it in any way.

The best thing that anyone ever said was just the word 'time'. A couple of people have just said, 'Time', to me and it's perfect because, really, that's all you have. Time encapsulates my existence – I can't grasp anything else except for the fact that time is passing. Time goes on and, in time, something will happen. You just don't know what.

A lot of people have said more recently, 'You seem better.' They don't have a clue. Although, in a way it's true because for the first couple of weeks I even needed help tying my shoelaces, so I guess what they're trying to say now is that I seem better than I was then – more capable, more coherent. But then I feel under pressure to say, 'Yes, I'm OK', when really I'm not; I'm just better at pretending. So I try and convey this by responding with something like, 'Well, it's a bad day today, and yesterday was an awful day.'

I feel uncomfortable when people say things like, 'I know it's not the same but . . . ' Then I find myself listening to a completely incomparable story about something that truly doesn't matter to me in the grand scheme of things. These people's stories couldn't be further from what has happened to me, and while I appreciate that they are trying to help, it just makes me want to shut down.

The phrase 'be strong' is also an odd one. It's a ludicrous statement. It doesn't mean anything, nor does it help in any way. How can one possibly 'be strong'? I feel I am in the middle of a nervous breakdown, and the words 'be strong' imply that what's happened is insignificant – that if I could just be strong, I'd be OK. It makes no sense!

What Helped – and What Didn't?

I don't tend to break down in front of many people. I feel I can gauge those who just wouldn't know what to do and that makes me quite guarded – and it doesn't help them to help me either. The people who can't handle it make themselves known to you very quickly – they just won't be there.

I do a lot of hugging and that's very important, but sometimes you don't want any interaction at all. There have been times when I've been hugged and I haven't hugged back.

Most of the time I'm so wrapped up in the fact that I haven't got my partner any more that I don't notice if someone cries with me; I'm just focusing on expelling my own pain. But I comforted my mum the other day when she cried, and it was a total role reversal. I just stood there telling her, 'It's OK', and felt I was trying to tell myself that too. I wanted to listen to my own advice. But it's very difficult. When you see someone else's pain you think, 'Christ if that's your pain, imagine what mine is'. I've said that before to Mum and some friends in an attempt to get them to understand.

I try to let people know that even though time has gone by, I'm not OK. It's a reminder that yes, I'm still here, but don't go away. The best thing someone can do is to give me their time – to listen to me, to talk to me, to be there. I will never forget the people who have given me their time.

One moment that stands out is when I went back into the chapel of rest for the third time to see my beautiful Lizzie. When I came out, the funeral director placed his hand on my shoulder and asked me with sincere concern, 'Are you OK?' It was just the most poignant human attempt at reaching out. He was looking at a person who had just lost their partner and could see that I clearly wasn't OK, but the way he asked me – with such recognition of my state – brought me out of myself. He must see that every day, yet he took the time to check on me.

For the funeral, Lizzie's mum asked me what I thought of her choice of coffin – I was grateful for that – and I was in the family car and did a reading, but I wasn't involved in organising anything, which in some ways is very upsetting. I didn't help with packing her stuff up either, and I found that hard, but I didn't feel I could ask to have a look. I have accepted that Lizzie's at home, her things are at home, and that's where they must belong.

One friend suggested I write things down. That was a good idea. He also said he thought that sometimes I might need to just listen to him talking to me. That was actually really nice – to give my brain a rest and to hear someone else talking about something else. Now sometimes I text people and just say, 'What are you doing … Tell me.' I know it comes across as blunt, but I want them to give me something to take my mind off what I'm thinking. You have to find ways to take yourself away for a few seconds. That seems to work.

I like to think I'm known for being a nice chap, but that makes me feel there's an expectation for me to be cheery. And it feels like there is a time frame. The funeral seems to be a watershed in people's minds: for two weeks everyone was there every minute I needed them, but within two days of the funeral, people had got quieter. So if I was to say one thing, it would be that it gets worse after the funeral. That day you say goodbye, then that's it and things go downhill.

With family it's different though. With them, I can be whatever I need to be. I am very snappy with them and they take it – they know it's such a difficult time. But that's something I can't do with friends. With family, it's truly unconditional. My sister said she'd never seen me the way I was when Lizzie was lowered into the ground, but she didn't penalise or judge me for doing something out of character. She took it on board and got on with it.

I made a new friend. A girl who had lost her best friend some years before just came into my life, full of heart, and has checked in on me every day and shown so much support. It's amazing. She's the only person I felt comfortable sharing an experience of loss with because we had both lost a friend. She was also very honest about the vagueness of her understanding of what I was going through, and she just let me talk. There is never a time with her when I can't be totally honest and say, 'I feel like shit'.

I know my other friends are there, but life for them has moved on. And I'm the one who has stood still. As much as I'm annoyed and confused with the fact that people move on, they have to and I get that.

I haven't lost any friends, but some just haven't been present. They have backed away and spoken to me very little – or not at all. I think it is some people's way of dealing with it. They just don't know what to say. Or they may feel they don't have the time. Or it's a road they don't want to go down because they don't know what will be asked of them. I don't think any less of them for it. I'm just grateful for any time that people have given me. Time is precious.

And Lastly ...

It's all about just being there, in any shape or form; to talk, to listen, to be present in some way. The best thing you can do is give them some of your life that is purely for them.

What you can learn from Ben's story

If a friend loses a partner when they have been together for only a few years, it clearly has implications on the space that's left for them within the family of the deceased. Ultimately they lose their place because the death somehow excommunicates them from the family system. So you'll need to be there for them even more.

Be careful of how you respond to the 'good days'. It's rather like only praising a child when they get A grades in school; pretty soon they'll learn that that is the only way to get love. Equally, a bereaved person, especially someone like Ben who knows he's thought of as a nice guy, could start to become a pleaser, and feel like there is no room for the messiness and ugliness that comes with grief.

Finally, the bereaved develop a script they read to make things comfortable for the non-bereaved when they ask about it. If you're a close friend, don't be fooled by it. At the very least, tell them you've heard that script before and give them the opportunity to chuck it to one side. It may be that they don't feel prepared or safe enough to let it go, but at least they know they don't have to follow it for your sake.

Chapter 17

What the experts say

Reading through the various stories in this book will, hopefully, have given you a sense of how people feel in the immediate wake of bereavement and beyond. However, as I pointed out in the Introduction, no two people are alike in their experience of grief, and so while you might have picked up some tips as to what may be useful (and not so useful) when it comes to helping your bereaved friend or loved one, you will probably have noticed that there are also some recurring contradictions running through the stories. In this chapter I'm going to explore some of these similarities and contradictions and consider what they can teach us about the nature of grief. I have also included the thoughts of experts from organisations working in bereavement and palliative care: CRUSE, St Christopher's Hospice, Grief Encounter and Dying Matters (for more information about these, see Resources, page 191).

Indulgence versus Avoidance

Perhaps one particularly stark contrast that has emerged is that some people appear to *identify* with their loss (i.e. express it, talk about it, cry about it), while others *detach* from it (i.e. go straight back to work and – seemingly – 'get on' with life). Through both my research for this book and my own personal experience, I have found that society's approach to death has forged the myth that the stiff-upper-lip response is a sign of strength; people often assume that those who take the distraction route are 'dealing well' with their bereavement and need less help than those who cry a lot and appear to be 'wallowing'. Indeed, I have found myself making this judgement at times, on others and on myself, and the impact of denying and avoiding my own pain was very destructive. In order to provide effective support to the bereaved, this myth has to be crushed – it is so important that others do not impose their own judgements as to what they think would be best or how they might do things differently.

Renowned professors Stroebe and Schut at Utrecht University in the Netherlands identified the dual process model of coping with bereavement, whereby people go back and forth between the experience of *loss* (sadness, anger, yearning, crying, denial) and that of *restoration* (sorting things out, feeling 'normal', joy, contentment, laughing, adapting). The key point to take from this is that both kinds of activities – the loss- or indulgence-based, as well as the restoration- or avoidance-based – are very important for healing, and the bereaved may oscillate between the two from the beginning of the process and throughout. As Stroebe and Schut put it: 'Bereaved individuals need times when they face their grief and times when they look to the future and avoid it. Both too much and too little grief can be harmful.'

I found their description of bouncing back and forth between these two methods of coping enormously helpful in understanding my own shifts in mourning and also when hearing the experiences of others. Each side of the grief coin requires different types of support, and so it can be difficult to keep up or know which is required and when; but in just approaching the grieving person with this in mind, you will be much better placed to adapt and respond appropriately.

> *'Each individual should be allowed and encouraged to grieve in whatever way feels most comfortable to them, providing they are not at risk of self-harming/harming others. It is important to remember that a person may think they are delaying the grief and getting on with life, but grief cannot be denied and will resurface in the future. Friends should encourage the bereaved person to not feel weak or foolish for showing emotions and likewise remind the bereaved person it is OK to laugh at a joke or to not think constantly about the person who has died.'*
>
> Alison Thompson, CRUSE

> *'The people who tend to be over-controlled in their grief are often those that friends don't worry about as they seem to be "coping" so well; however they may have other symptoms of grief, such as physical problems and stress.'*
>
> Bereavement Team, St Christopher's Hospice

It's clear then, that as supporter to someone recently bereaved, it's important not to encourage one mode of coping more than the other. And further, if you identify your friend as being either one or the other, don't be surprised if they suddenly switch to behaving in the opposite way. Let there be space for it all. The St Christopher's experts also bring our attention to the importance of keeping a keen eye on your bereaved friend. Look out for signs of the grief in more subtle manifestations. They may not cry very often, and perhaps they have gone back to work smoothly and swiftly, but are they sleeping? Are they eating? What is their mood like generally? All these things can be warning signals that something is being repressed and is eating away at your friend in an invisible but profound way.

Physical Affection

People have different views about physical contact when they are grieving. For some people a hug is a failsafe response in times of crisis – as Norman says on page 145–6, a hug 'tells you all you need to know', but for others such as Julia in Chapter 6, a hug can feel uncomfortable and even intrusive. They often do more for the comforter than the bereaved. So perhaps there is room for a little more care and thought with the use of hugs.

> *'Hugging is a normal need for anyone who is feeling uncared for and vulnerable; however, most of us feel inhibited in receiving a hug depending on who is offering this and in what setting, and it can make a person feel more vulnerable still.'*
>
> Bereavement Team, St Christopher's Hospice

Some people can be sensitive to whom it is they receive a hug from. Just because you know someone who has been recently bereaved, don't assume they will be more needy or receptive of hugs, especially if you are not particularly close. Try and read their body language. I remember I would be particularly smiley and move around a lot if I didn't want to be hugged. Look out for whether they appear guarded? Arms crossed? Or can you sense an openness in their vulnerability? How close do they get to you or allow you to come to them?

Most hugs are offered when the bereaved person starts crying.

There may well be times when this hug is exactly what the person needs to completely let go and melt into the emotions they're experiencing. But at other times it can feel like a distraction from the pain. And as surprising as it sounds, it can feel like your friend is trying to 'muzzle' you, to cover up your tears. Don't launch in with a hug as soon as you see your friend, especially if they are crying. Look them in the eyes, squeeze their shoulders, see if they are reaching out to be held, or if actually they just need space. Encourage them to trust that the helplessness of the moment makes no difference to your ability to be with them.

Weeping

The poet Dannie Abse once said after his wife died: 'I cry therefore I am.'

In Chapter 15 Lina spoke in detail about how important crying has been for her own expression of grief, but added that she often found herself having to prepare the supporter for her tears, so they didn't try to 'fix' her or disengage. It's sad this has to happen. What is it about this very human physical manifestation of emotion that makes some people feel so uncomfortable and nervous? It might help to know that very often crying is the best comfort that there is for the bereaved. My brother told me that when he cried he often felt his most connected to Mum and so it became something he was relieved to do, indeed something he wanted to do more. Those tears are a reflection of the pain of loss, and it's when we connect to that pain that we are truly feeling in relationship with the person we've lost. So keep this in mind the next time you find yourself tensing up at the sight of your friends tears. Share in the sense of relief and release they may be experiencing and let them be.

Of course, not everyone cries in mourning. And some people, such as Norman in Chapter 14, were acutely aware that tears are often seen as proof of someone processing grief to outsiders. Use your intuition. It might be that they want to cry but genuinely can't and so being encouraged or asked about it might be frustrating and evoke a sense of failure. If they look like they are trying to hold in the tears, accept that you can't force them, but perhaps gently ask if they feel able to let them out in private at least or if there are other places/circumstances they feel safe enough to cry.

> 'Crying can convey lots of different emotions and should be allowed as any other expression; but it might also help for the bereaved to reflect on what they are expressing in this crying. Also, offering a packet or box of tissues too readily could be interpreted as, "Hurry up and stop crying – you're making me feel uncomfortable." People need time to cry.'
>
> Bereavement Team, St Christopher's Hospice

Whether or not your friend expresses themselves with tears will be influenced by a variety of factors, including their upbringing, culture, and whether they feel safe in each given moment. Try to take these into consideration when you are with your friend or loved one, and don't be too quick to judge the meaning of their tears or lack thereof. If indeed they do cry with you, don't immediately hand them tissues or smother them with a hug. Our tendency when we cry is to hold our breath, so encourage them to keep breathing as this will keep the flow of the emotion going. This will in turn assure them that you aren't frightened by their sobs.

* * *

As well as the evident contradictions between the various stories in the book, there are also certain themes that many contributors focused on, even if they were experienced in different ways.

Time

Time is curious. It's so fundamental to our day-to-day living, and yet it is so abstract: it is a thing we give to people; it is something we spend; and, especially when we have gone through some kind of trauma, it is something we simply experience. We sit through it and wait for it to pass. For Ben, in Chapter 16, time was the only concrete thing he could hold on to and so for this to be mirrored was a great comfort. However, for others time stops existing. I could barely tell the difference between today or tomorrow, daytime and night time. It stopped mattering. Molly in Chapter 2 talks of how painful it was knowing that time was passing and that each day meant she was experiencing things that Felix would never know about. I too didn't want time to continue. I wanted to be as close to the time of Mum's death as possible. It seemed to me that it would mean I was closer to her being alive.

This sense that time stands still, or slows down was experienced by many of the contributors. As a result, daily functioning and experiencing life happened at a much slower pace than normal. Reactions to things people say are sluggish, daily activities, such as getting dressed and deciding what to have for breakfast, seem to take enormous effort, as concentration lessens. It's as though the internal clock, and speed at which the person operates, goes into slow motion. Here again then, the surrounding supporters need to mirror this, or at least develop the patience to work around it.

'*While grieving people seem to need to process the events and circumstances and the implications of the loss – and while they undertake this cognitive and emotional task they are often very preoccupied. This leads to them being less able to concentrate on things, possibly feeling slower and more faltering with ordinary everyday tasks that they would usually manage. People also experience grief as over-whelmingly tiring, which may lead to feeling things are slowing down. Again, those around the grieving person need to factor in that the person will get tired quicker, have less stamina and less concentration.*'

Bereavement Team, St Christopher's Hospice

'*Again this is a common reaction that many bereaved people experience following the death of someone close. Some symptoms of grief can resemble a major depressive episode, which can leave the individual feeling as if everything is slowing down around them. At present, psychiatrists and other clinicians are undecided as to whether the presence of feeling "slowed down" is indicative of "normal grief" or depression triggered by the grief as a secondary symptom.*''

Alison Thompson, CRUSE

People also grieve for an incredibly long time. Some would say forever. This can be a challenge for supporters as it can exclude them from feeling a part of the process. On the day Mum died, I remember knowing instantly that I had just entered into a process that I would experience in total isolation because it was going to take longer than anyone could comprehend. That was a rather frightening thought and my way of coping was to assign myself a year in which to do it – that way, I could warn people to expect that that was how long I'd be grieving for. I rather shot myself in the foot though because for much of that first year I felt OK, and it wasn't until the early part of the second year that the agony really started rising to the surface, by which point, of course, most people had stopped asking about it.

> '*It is not uncommon for people who have never been bereaved to assume a perceived time frame for grieving to end and for the mourner to "get back to normal". However, most people who have been bereaved will understand that the ways in which a person grieves and for how long will be unique to them. If the bereaved person remains stuck within their grief for over six months without regression or progression, professional intervention may also be required.*'
>
> Alison Thompson, CRUSE

The important point to take from Alison Thompson's advice is to look out for movement in the way your friend or loved one is grieving, rather than improvement. Just as we saw through the dual process model, the process of grief doesn't occur as a smooth transition from wounding to healing. It goes back and forth. But if you feel that your friend is somehow stuck, and has been for over six months, then it might be that some professional support would be helpful for them.

Unpredictable Behaviour

Lots of people highlighted contradictions in their own behaviour when reliving their experience of grief and loss. Rose talked, for example, of wanting her friends to treat her normally one minute, and the next being frustrated they weren't asking her about her brother. And on page 93 Anna describes how a letter arriving on one day might be received in a totally different way at another time. This obviously presents a rather big challenge for the supporter. How can you manage the unpredictable nature of the bereaved life-state? The important thing to remember is that none of these feelings are more right or real than the others. They are all true to that person in that moment. This requires energy and preparation on your part, so that you can adapt to whatever is required in each instance, and also so that you don't take offence when a tactic that worked yesterday isn't so effective today. It's not you; it's them!

> 'The mourner is often trying to both accept and deny grief simultaneously and, as such, their thought processes and emotional responses can appear erratic. Where the bereaved person is on their grief journey and how they are adjusting to their loss can significantly affect whether external distractions, such as the arrival of friends, will be welcomed or not. Friends of the bereaved person should be reminded that the death of someone close is a traumatic and extremely painful event and they should be encouraged not to take any angry outbursts, refusals to be seen or requests to leave, personally.'
>
> Alison Thompson, CRUSE

There isn't really a simple solution to this characteristic of the bereaved. As and when it feels appropriate, check in with them, ask them what has been helpful and if they think they'd like more of that. But don't hold them to it too tightly. The best thing you can do is to stay open-minded and avoid too much forward planning.

Repetition

Many people said that they wanted to share their experience of grief with friends again and again, and often each time it could feel as though it was being said for the first time. Even three years on, I still appreciate any chance I get to tell someone about the day Mum died. It is such a catastrophic experience that talking about it repeatedly feels simultaneously like bringing them back to life while comprehending their deadness.

> *'By repeating the story the grieving person is endeavouring to make sense of the death, looking for answers to questions they feel need answering. Telling the story repeatedly allows the bereaved person to frame how they are feeling and where they are within their grief. Unless the reliving is causing continued and increasing disruption to the bereaved person's daily life, friends should allow them to go over what has happened and how they feel as much as they need to.'*

Alison Thompson, CRUSE

> *'The effect of the trauma often leads to them distancing themselves from the event and it can cause splits in their feelings, thoughts and behaviours, which may mean they need to tell the story over and over again. It's important to allow space for them to tell their story, especially in the early days, so they can begin to find a way of coming to terms with their new reality. And also so they can maintain a connection with the dead person while moving on with their lives. Friends can support them by adding their thoughts and feelings as well.'*

Shelley Gilbert, Grief Encounter

Don't be alarmed if you notice that your friend or loved one is repeating themselves and is seemingly unaware they are doing so. It's not a sign of madness, simply a reflection of the pace at which the person can process what they've just experienced, and perhaps also their way of sharing it with you. The key thing is to sustain a good listening ear. It's understandable that you might find it rather difficult hearing the gory details again and again, or perhaps you're bored of hearing about what the deceased was wearing when they died, or what so and so said at the funeral. But try and bear it in mind that for the mourner it will feel like the first time they're saying it. Joy in Chapter 13 touches on how grateful she still feels now to hear of people asking after her husband. Don't switch off the minute you hear your friend tell you something you already know, make the effort to concentrate and express interest by asking questions. Show you are willing to keep exploring their new reality with them.

Language and Communication

It is worth thinking quite carefully about the language you use with your bereaved friend or loved one. Beatrice in Chapter 3 said how important it was to call a death a death. I remember finding it very frustrating when people asked about my mum's 'passing'. The fact that there are over 200 euphemisms for the word 'died' serves as a very clear demonstration of just how uncomfortable we are with talking openly about death. The more we pander to these, the less confident we will feel in the company of the bereaved.

Being straightforward with your language is important when supporting younger bereaved people too. Bereaved children are commonly much more comfortable speaking very frankly about death. When I trained for the child bereavement service at St Christopher's Hospice, we did multiple role plays to practise telling small children that dead bodies *rot*, and that cremation is when the bodies are *burned*. Everyone found it incredibly challenging to imagine talking to these little vulnerable people using such brutal words, but the fear was all our own; kids can handle it.

> 'In my work with bereaved children and young people I often find that they have not been given the opportunity to tell the story of what has happened from their point of view. They may have been "told" what has happened but rarely asked more than once how they feel. They need explicit support in the form of acknowledgement, information, appraisal and active interventions and they need to hear in your words that you feel OK talking to them about it.'
>
> Shelley Gilbert, Grief Encounter

So it's not only about the words you use, it's about the way in which you respond to your friend or loved one. Follow their lead with language and listen out for clues, especially with the younger bereaved. They may be waiting for you to create the space for them to explore their feelings further.

The different channels we use to communicate also emerged as a theme in some of the contributors' stories. Nicola in Chapter 8 talks of how differently she experienced support because it was pre-mobile phone and social media time. It was easier to hide from the bereaved then, but it's not so simple now. There are fewer excuses for not getting in touch. Having said that, this may not be the case for people of all ages. For the younger generation, communicating by text or email comes as naturally as walking. But this may not be the default mode for some people. Don't send a long personal email to someone who isn't a regular emailer. And I'd suggest, even for those who are, don't assume they will be checking. Daily tasks such as checking emails are often forgotten in the early days of a bereavement so make sure you get in touch using a number of different channels. I doubt there would be many cases where going the extra mile would be unwelcome. If you do write to your friend or loved one, especially to people of an older generation, tell them it is not necessary for them to respond. For older bereaved people, the obligation to reply will be invoked, so remind them you are not expecting to hear back.

> 'For many people, the increasing range of online and social media options available allows them to engage in discussions about dying, death and bereavement more easily, which is a really positive development. However, it's important to remember that not everyone is online and that significant numbers of people would still much rather talk face to face about such important issues, either instead of or as well as through email, text or social media. It's therefore essential to take time to choose your mode of communication to be mindful both of what you want to say and the best way of saying it.'
>
> Joe Levenson,
> Director of Communications, Dying Matters Coalition

Hierarchy of Grief

Many of the people I spoke to would preface their story with something like, 'I know it's not as bad as if I'd lost a child/parent' or, 'I know it would have been worse if they'd been murdered'. There seems to be a hierarchy of grief, which impacts on how much support people feel they have a right to expect. Adam in Chapter 7 lost two people, and they were murdered. Harry in Chapter 12 lost his father to suicide. These deaths may feel to some a greater loss than others. But Adam himself makes the point that it was important for his friends to acknowledge that the greatest loss was actually that of the parents.

While I would agree with Adam, this is not necessarily a universally shared core belief. And it is certainly not something one should say to someone who has lost their parent or sibling as some attempt to put their experience into perspective. However, be mindful that, rightly or wrongly, there is some sense of hierarchy in our collective unconscious and the different types of loss, and the relationship the person had with the deceased, may influence what your friend or loved one needs from you.

'No death is better or worse than another, and although Western society appears to favour natural orders of death for example children outlive their parents, death is life-altering for every bereaved person. Better than colluding in the assumptions of society, friends and family should listen to the bereaved person, share their pain and enable them to grieve safely and in ways appropriate to them.'

Alison Thompson, CRUSE

'It appears that someone can grieve in such a way that they can have problems continuing with other aspects to their lives, following the death of someone that others might feel could have been expected. This 'disenfranchised grief' (grief not acknowledged by society) can be hard for the bereaved

to express as they feel others don't understand the enormous impact it has had on them. Or someone can lose a child, say, or experience a traumatic death such as through suicide, and this might have the opposite effect, with family and friends so unsure as to what they should say that they may then make the bereaved feel more isolated by their loss.'

Bereavement Team, St Christopher's Hospice

The challenge then is to achieve a balance between acknowledging the gravity of your friend or loved one's unique loss, while not isolating them by making them feel that their loss is incomparable, as this can feed into them feeling totally incapable of ever returning to 'normal'. Test it out with them – try and uncover whether it's actually helpful for their loss to be the worst, or if they find comfort in being part of a shared process.

Family System

The family set-up or structure can have a profound influence on your bereaved friend's experience of grief, particularly if they are younger. In my case, losing my mum when my parents were already separated meant that long-term responsibilities, such as managing the house and taking care of the dog, inevitably fell to my brother and me almost immediately. Although of course we were supported by our dad, had he lived with us, we might have gotten away with 'leaving it all to the grown up' as Nicola, in Chapter 8 was indeed encouraged to do. Take these factors into consideration when deciding how best you can support your friend or loved one. Are they suddenly having to ring up lots of companies and inform them of the death and change names on utilities, and have tax people come round and value things, clear out clothes cupboards and so on? Can you help them with these tasks? What responsibilities are going to fall on to them? Be prepared that if they are younger or more isolated, they may depend on you more.

> *'If a child loses a parent who does not live with them, their living arrangements mostly do not change, and therefore often things will appear to carry on as 'normal' without giving themselves (or being given) the acknowledgement or space to process the grief associated with the loss of a parent. It can be a very lonely and isolating place to be. Realise they are not the same person any more and help them become that different but stronger person. Do not be afraid to go to dark places with them and help them to remember, not to forget.*
>
> *In cases where your friend has lost the parent they lived with, home is often no longer the safe, comforting place that it had been before. Although we may all want to wear the Best Friend badge in the beginning, it will be very hard to maintain, especially as most of what your friend is going through will be beyond comprehension. Help them find a community (not just on Facebook) where they can be with others who have experienced the premature death of a parent. This will help with the transition to the new life they will now have to live, and reassure them they are not alone.'*
>
> Shelley Gilbert, Grief Encounter

Shelley Gilbert's point draws our attention to grief in younger children, and she crucially points out the importance of not assuming the death of an absent parent will be less impactful than that of the parent who lives at home. Harry's experience in

Chapter 12 is a clear example of just how complex family dynamics can be and how this in turn affects the experience of grief. The separation of your parents is hard enough for children, it's a loss in itself, so be conscious of this with your young bereaved friend or loved one. It might mean they feel less able to talk about it at home if the parent they live with is not experiencing the loss as intensely as they are. Make sure you create space for them to grieve when they are with you, if they appear to want to. Think creatively about how you can support them in making sense of what's happened – memory boxes, photo albums, writing stories, drawing pictures; all these can be wonderfully healing ways to share your friend's burden of loss and help them maintain a sense of connection to the deceased.

Chapter 18

Dos and Don'ts

Grief sorts people out . . . as the survivor's life is
forcibly recalibrated, friendships are often tested;
some pass, some fail.

Julian Barnes

DO *offer to do something specific.*

Before you make contact or go to see the bereaved person, perhaps think about them and their personal circumstances and
how you can tailor any help to their particular needs. Do you live
near them? Do you enjoy cooking? Do they have children/pets
that need looking after? Then just go ahead and tell them you are
going to be helping them with a certain task. If they tell you
outright, 'No thank you', then that's fine, and they will still
appreciate that you thought about them; but if they offer the
obligatory protest, ignore it and go ahead with your suggestion.

DO *ask them questions about their loss.*

Again – discretion is required here, but it's important to remember that questions about the pain, the dead person, the

experience are not necessarily out of bounds. Chapter 16 is a good example of how positive this kind of curiosity can be. Perhaps check if it's OK to ask a question about it and go from there. The bereaved often want to tell the story over and over again, so to have someone take an interest might well be an enormous comfort.

DO *make a joke about the awkwardness of the situation.*

If the bereaved person seems to be in a jokey mood, join in. Grief doesn't kill sense of humour; in fact, it can often heighten it in some ways, so bring them some relief with jokes, and don't let the death become the elephant in the room.

DO *share memories of the dead person ... in letters and conversation.*

This is a great thing to do, particularly in letters. Very often the bereaved feel more alone in their loss, so hearing that others are sad about it can be very consoling. That's not to say that you should focus exclusively on your own pain and how hard it is going to be for you – just that you could express an awareness of how awful it is that they are dead and that you know you will miss certain things about them.

DO *remain consistent in your behaviour.*

Almost everyone in this book spoke somewhere about wanting their friends to be their normal selves with them. Try and be you, as much as you can – but just a you who is there more than usual.

DO *be honest.*

The best thing in any situation is to be honest, and this applies as much to supporting the bereaved as it does to anything else. So if you don't know what to say, you're not sure what to do or you don't know what to write – just relax for a minute and then be truthful with yourself and the person who is in mourning.

DON'T *make it about you and your experience of grief.*

Take this as a general rule of thumb. There will, of course, be times when the bereaved person wants to hear of your experience, but wait for them to ask you.

DON'T *send commercial 'sympathy' cards with generic poems in them. Write something personal.*

This might seem like a small point, but the effect can be considerable. Even if they don't remember the contents of your letter an hour after opening it, the experience of receiving it, reading it and seeing the thought and kindness that have gone into it will bring someone far more comfort than a standard card. You don't have to write masses, but bring your 'Self' into the letter. This can be hard if you are not close to the person, but you can say, simply, that although you didn't know the deceased, or indeed, the bereaved very well, you are still thinking about them and feel truly sad for their loss. If you do know the person well, then demonstrate it.

DON'T *try to stop someone crying.*

Never tell someone, 'Oh don't cry'. As has already been mentioned, crying is not only cathartic but can be incredibly healing in that it often brings the bereaved closer to their deceased loved one. Don't make these opportunities unavailable just because of your own discomfort.

DON'T *think that everything will be OK once the funeral is over.*

As was mentioned in Chapter 10, if you can, be prepared to get more involved after the first month. That's when things often really start to crumble and when most people start to drift. So send another letter, suggest an activity, keep them occupied and surrounded. Equally, if you weren't around at the time of death and several years have passed, get in touch. It is *never* too late to tell someone you are thinking of them. But perhaps don't expect a reply.

DON'T *rely on others to be there.*

If you know a bereaved person who doesn't appear to have many friends – make more of an effort. Don't rely on people to be there. People who don't ordinarily have a lot of people around them might well be used to it, but that doesn't mean they won't need them when the time comes.

Resources

UK

CRUSE

CRUSE Bereavement is the largest and perhaps best-known bereavement charity in the UK. It has been running for over fifty years and offers face-to-face and group support, as well as online help and a telephone helpline. They also provide training to organisations and individuals who work with bereaved people.

Telephone: 0844 477 9400
www.cruse.org.uk

Dying Matters

Dying Matters is a national coalition of 30,000 members, which aims to change public knowledge, attitudes and behaviours towards dying, death and bereavement. It was set up by the National Council for Palliative Care (NCPC) in 2009 and its members include organisations from across the NHS, voluntary and independent health and care sectors, social care and housing sectors, a wide range of faith organisations, community organisations, schools and colleges and the funeral sector, as well as individuals like myself.

Telephone: 0800 021 44 66
www.dyingmatters.org

Grief Encounter

Grief Encounter is one of the UK's leading child bereavement charities. It was set up in 2003 by Shelley Gilbert, who, tragically, had lost both her parents by the age of nine. It provides pioneering services such as the 'Family Programme', which includes one-to-one counselling, workshops, books, a Grief Relief Kit, residential camp and family days. Grief Encounter also offers a variety of specialist resources, an interactive website and a range of award-winning publications.

Telephone: 0208 371 8455
http://www.griefencounter.org.uk/

Macmillan Cancer Support

Provide practical, medical and financial support not only for patients but also for those caring for someone with terminal cancer and the bereaved.

Telephone: 0808 808 00 00
www.macmillan.org.uk

St Christopher's Hospice

Founded by Dame Cicely Saunders in 1967, St Christopher's

Hospice, in turn, kick-started the modern hospice movement. Saunders' philosophy was, 'You matter because you are you ... and you matter to the last moment of your life.' St Christopher's is one of the largest hospice services in the UK and exists to promote and provide skilled and compassionate palliative care of the highest quality. Having seen their work at first hand, I can say with complete conviction that they are extraordinarily good at what they do.

Telephone: 0208 768 4500
www.stchristophers.org.uk

Australia

Australian Centre for Grief and Bereavement

They have extensive online information on how to help the bereaved and provide workshops, a telephone helpline and training for professionals.

www.grief.org.au

Grieflink

This is an online information resource for the bereaved and those caring for the bereaved. They have some useful tips on what is helpful and not so helpful for supporting someone in mourning.

www.grieflink.asn.au

New Zealand

Skylight

They offer a wide range of services to support those facing change, loss, trauma and grief, whatever the cause and whatever their age.

www.skylight.org.nz

Grief Centre

They provide support, advice and counselling to anyone affected by loss and grief. They have a number of resources giving information on different types of loss.

www.griefcentre.org.nz

South Africa

Khululeka Grief Support

They create supportive environments for bereaved children through training anyone who works with them.

www.khululeka.org

The Compassionate Friends of Cape Town

Non-profit support group for anyone trying to cope with the loss of a child of any age.

www.tcfcape.co.za

Spain

AMAD – Association Mutual Aid to the Grieving

An organisation which runs weekly support groups for the bereaved and provides advice for friends of the bereaved on how to help.

www.amad.es

Duelia

A social network which helps the bereaved through online support groups. You can either help or be a helper and you can choose who you'd like to be supported by. It also offers direct contact with bereavement professionals and psychotherapists.

www.duelia.org

USA

Grief Share

A ministry of the Church Initiative – this is a network of bereaved people and bereavement professionals which run weekly groups and seminars on a local basis. You simply put in your postcode and turn up at your local group.

www.griefshare.org
Telephone: (international) 919 562 2122

Center for Loss

An organisation supporting people in mourning, friends of the bereaved and bereavement professionals. Run by Dr Alan Wolfelt, Center for Loss helps those who are grieving by walking with them in their unique journey, and serves as educational resource to professional and lay caregivers.

www.centerforloss.com
Telephone: 970 226 6050

Bibliography

The Presence, Dannie Abse (Hutchinson, 2007)

Levels of Life, Julian Barnes (Jonathan Cape, 2013)

Death, Grief and Mourning, Geoffrey Gorer (Cresset Press, 1965)

Essays on life and death, Daisaku Ikeda (from an essay series by Daisaku Ikeda first published in the Philippines magazine *Mirror*, 1998)

A Grief Observed, C. S. Lewis (Faber and Faber, 1961)

Handbook of Bereavement Research, Margaret S. Strobe and Henk Schut (American Psychological Association, 2001)

'Modern Death: Taboo or not Taboo', Tony Walter (SAGE Journals, *Sociology*, May 1991, 25: 293–310)

Existential Therapy, Dr Irvin Yalom (Basic Books, 1980)